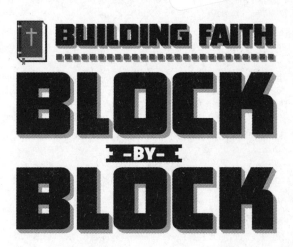

BUILDING FAITH
BLOCK
-BY-
BLOCK

MICHAEL ROSS
CHRISTOPHER ROSS

HARVEST
kids™

HARVEST KIDS is a registered trademark of The Hawkins Children's LLC. Harvest House Publishers, Inc., is the exclusive licensee of the federally registered trademark HARVEST KIDS.

Cover illustration and design by Kyler Dougherty

Interior design by Janelle Coury

Published in association with WordServe Literary Group, Ltd., www.wordserveliterary.com

BUILDING FAITH BLOCK BY BLOCK

Copyright © 2017 Michael Ross and Christopher Ross
Published by Harvest House Publishers
Eugene, Oregon 97402
www.harvesthousepublishers.com

Library of Congress Cataloging-in-Publication Data
Names: Ross, Michael, 1961- author. | Ross, Christopher, 2002- author.
Title: Building faith block by block / Michael Ross and Christopher Ross.
Description: Eugene, Oregon : Harvest House Publishers, [2017]
Identifiers: LCCN 2016053087 (print) | LCCN 2017007325 (ebook) | ISBN 9780736970853 (pbk.) | ISBN 9780736970860 (e-book)
Subjects: LCSH: Christian children—Religious life—Juvenile literature. | Christian children—Conduct of life—Juvenile literature. | Christian children—Prayers and devotions—Juvenile literature. | Minecraft (Game)—Miscellanea—Juvenile literature.
Classification: LCC BV4571.3 .R67 2017 (print) | LCC BV4571.3 (ebook) | DDC 248.8/2—dc23
LC record available at https://lccn.loc.gov/2016053087

Printed in the United States of America

17 18 19 20 21 22 23 24 25 / VP-JC / 10 9 8 7 6 5 4 3 2 1

For Tiffany
We love you...and have so much fun
sharing this amazing Minecrafty world with you!

CONTENTS

Unlock the Fun!

I bolt out of bed and squint in the darkness.

Something woke me up—sort of an eerie moan...or maybe it was a growl. *Zombies! Bet they're outside my front door. Maybe an army of them.*

Suddenly...*HHHIIISSSSS...CLANG!* Something is *inside* my house, and I can detect faint scampering sounds moving up and down my walls.

Spiders!

But I can't see a thing. Every torch in my house has gone out—including the ones on my porch. *This is bad!*

"Lenny," I call out to my ocelot-turned-cuddly cat. (The Minecraft tutorial I watched online was right on: Feed a wild ocelot three fish, and it will turn into a cute cat.) "Hey, crazy pet...my favorite four-legged friend who would never in a million, zillion years leave a Minecraft pal in the dark to fend for himself, *where are you*? I'm really scared and—"

I stop midsentence. I hear noises coming from the long corridor that leads to my mine.

I run my hand over the spot where my cat usually sleeps but make contact with nothing but a dead fish! At least my cat has been here. "Lenny," I yell a little louder. "Lenny, come here!" At this point my orange-and-brown-spotted friend usually greets me with an arched back and a face full of imaginary cat kisses. But this time...silence.

I quietly open a storage chest next to my bed and pull out my trusty bow and arrow. I raise them high in the air, ready to fire, and then take a quick peek out my front window. Nothing but darkness. Not the monster freak show I imagined on my doorstep.

Yep—I definitely have visitors in my mine. It's go time!

As I make my way toward the noises, I can't help but groan at my surroundings. I crafted this place with a pickaxe and my own two virtual hands, but when night falls and the monsters roam, my house begins to feel more creepy than cool. There are cold gray stones everywhere, and one of the walls is lined with stained glass windows—which, at the moment, look hauntingly eerie with moonlight shining through them.

What was I thinking? Why did I make this place look like a vampire's lair?

It reminds me of scary evenings in the real world. If I watch something spooky on TV before going to bed, I lie awake, shaking under the covers...wondering if that big pile of clothes Mom told me to pick up is going to form arms and legs and eventually attack me.

I take a step but nearly trip. Another one of Lenny's fish treats just slimed my floor. I squeeze shut my eyes and take a deep breath. "Lenny," I whisper to myself, "I need you now!" My heart is playing keyboards with my ribcage.

I take another step...followed by a fourth and a fifth...and I eventually reach the entrance to my mine. Directly in front of me is a long, narrow shaft that drops into the ground. A wooden ladder is the only way down.

"Torches," I whisper to myself. "They're still lit." A warm glow emanates from the opening. I stand perfectly still, just like a ninja. I hug a wall and listen intently. I hear desperate sounds—muffled growling and hissing coming from below.

I roll my head slightly and look into the pit.

"Lenny!" I spot my faithful pet on a ledge just a few feet down, poised for action—his tail all puffed out and his claws ready to strike.

GROWL...HHHIIISSSSS...WHOOSH!

I turn away to think about what I just saw: *My cat is attacking something, but what? Zombies aren't scared of cats, and neither are spiders. And the game makers haven't yet introduced monster mice. This means one thing: My faithful buddy is fighting a...*

"Creeper!"

Creepers are the most dangerous monsters in the game. They run toward their victims and explode, destroying just about everything in sight—especially players. But for some unknown reason, they fear cats and ocelots.

I've met plenty of creepers at school. But the kind I'm talking about are disguised as bad attitudes and ugly behaviors: envy, hatred, jealously, rage, selfishness, fear. They invade the hearts of otherwise good people, wreaking havoc in their lives.

Just as I spin around again to get a handle on the action...*WHOOSH!*

A creeper races up the ladder right at me. I take aim. (Curiously, in spite of not having any arms, ugly green creepers are good with ladders.)

"That's it—keep coming," I shout, taunting him just a little. "A bit closer. Keep coming because you are absolutely, positively gonna be...toast!"

I pull back on my bowstring and let an arrow fly.

POW...a direct hit! I fire again and again...and the creeper freezes in midair. And then, in an instant, it vanishes into oblivion.

I let out my one-millionth sigh of relief. (Hopefully, my last one for the night.)

Another monster down. Another win for the good guys. And I survive to make my Minecrafty world a better place.

As for Lenny...he gets an extra fish treat!

My first few moments in Minecraft began at daybreak.

I was completely alone—single-player, survival mode. But once darkness fell, I quickly discovered a secret: *We are never truly alone.*

Unseen eyes are always watching. Hidden dangers are lurking in the shadows, so we've got to stay alert. This tip can keep us alive...in the game and in real life.

I'm Dragee90, and I can't wait to share more secrets. See the little duck in the image at the start of this chapter? That's me—my character. A bow-slinging, warrior duck to be exact. He's fearless in battle, faithful to his friends, and an amazing monster hunter. (He snagged an *achievement*—a high honor—from game makers for taking out that creeper.) My character is full of surprises too. You can't help but crack up laughing when he springs into action. But watch out—this crazy duck is on a mission!

Building Faith Block by Block is all about discovering our very own real-life mission. Just like the game, the real world is filled with bad guys and heroes, struggles and victories. And on any given day, we have *tons* of decisions to make. Without warning, we find ourselves smack in the middle of hair-raising predicaments, like fending off creepers in our brains (bad attitudes and behaviors), escaping the smelly slime of stupid choices, and avoiding the web's darkest places.

In the virtual world of Minecraft, our problems are solved with a simple *TAP, TAP, TAP* on a keyboard. We can switch to creative mode and shut out all the bad stuff. At that point, we're in control as we explore strange lands and create whatever we want...worry-free. The game makers don't force us to choose preplanned responses or to follow a bunch of rules. Instead, we get to make our own choices and just have fun being ourselves.

Guess what? We can have this kind of freedom in real life too.

No one can totally escape the pressures of everyday living and breathing, but the Creator of all things—the one and only God of the universe, our heavenly Father—loves us more than we can ever imagine. He promises to guide our steps right through the bad stuff. God has amazing dreams for us—an ultimate mission that leads to eternal life with Him. But He'll never, ever force us to follow Him.

It's up to us to make that choice.

In each of these short chapters, I give you a click-by-click report of my Minecrafty adventures, and I'll share some useful tips that can help in the game...and in life.

Let's not waste another second. You already know what

happens when the sun goes down in Minecraft, so let's get moving. I have a lot to show you!

T

CLICK...CLICK...CLICK.

There it is—the first thing I want you to see. That stone fortress perched high atop a ridge is my house. You stumbled around it in the dark with me, but here's how it looks in the daylight. Since my heritage goes back to Sweden, Ireland, and England, I decided to honor my family with a medieval-styled, Irish-Scandinavian chateau. (Even the queen would love it here!) It took hours to craft.

Gray and whitewashed stone, weather-worn wood, turrets with brown-and-red-tiled roofs, narrow windows and doors with arches...pretty cool, huh? The inside is still rustic with just a handful of rooms, a crafting table, a bed, and some chests to hold my stuff. Its coolest feature is the long passageway that leads to my mine. (Remember the stained glass?)

It's my own royal hideaway, what I proudly call Mount Quack. I started it in a hurry, just minutes after I arrived in my Minecraft world. You know the drill: We spawn into the game at daybreak, but we have only ten minutes to find food, gather resources, build shelter, and prepare for nightfall. We absolutely can't be stranded in the dark.

So I strategically placed Mount Quack on the highest point, a steep peak where I feel safe at night. And during the day, I can see practically the whole world.

Speaking of the world, take a look...

CLICK, CLICK.

I was lucky enough to be spawned in a dense jungle, technically called the Jungle M biome. Really, this place is just one huge, mountainous island with trees that reach into the clouds and jagged cliffs that plunge into the ocean. It's a lush green paradise with waterfalls and caves and beaches that remind me of an island in the Bahamas—only better. I think I could live here for real!

Brightly colored flowers and cocoa pods seem to spawn everywhere. And all around us is a tangled ceiling of leaves and vines, so thick you can barely see the sky. If you listen closely, you can almost hear the crazy choruses of chirps and yelps, whistles and whirrs. And don't forget the soothing roar of the ocean. *Ahhh*...island life!

The coolest thing about the Bahamas was getting to swim with a bottlenose dolphin named Shawn. He was huge—nine feet long and weighing 500 pounds! But the cool thing about my virtual island is my creeper-scaring cat named Lenny. I think he eats as much fish as Shawn!

Check out some other great critters...

CLICK.

This place is teeming with friendly animals that seem to appear out of nowhere. Ocelots (just like my cat), wolves, pigs, and goofy-looking chickens often scamper into the thick brush. (Yep, crazy chickens inhabit this island!)

My world is resource rich, and if you play this game much, you know how important that is. Everywhere I look, I spot useful items: trees, stone, water, sand, cactus, sugar cane. And mining has really paid off. In addition to good stuff like coal ore and granite, I've dug up emerald and diamond ore. I trade emeralds with villagers on the other side of the island, and I craft armor out of diamonds. I end up with a glistening turquoise outfit that keeps me stylin' in battle!

As for Mount Quack, I have big plans for my place. The exterior is cool, but the interior needs a good HGTV makeover. I envision just the basics. You know, simple touches that make Scandinavian chateaus very...uh...chateau-like: sprawling courtyards with fountains, an indoor pool, a library, an armory. Torches everywhere. Outside, I'm going to build giant walls and lookout towers for protection. Mount Quack will be a safe place, shutting out scary stuff. That is, every bad thing but creepers.

I haven't figured out how to fully escape these guys. They pop up when we least expect them, and they're hard to beat. Thankfully, I have my cat, Lenny, by my side.

So there you have it—my Minecrafty world, fresh from my imagination!

Enough with the tour. Let's jump back into gameplay...this time multiplayer, survival mode. Sure, we'll switch back to creative mode from time to time to work on some mind-boggling Minecraft creations. But I really want you to join me in an A-to-Z quest for survival secrets. There's a lot we're going to discover together.

We'll mine some of the best-ever tips on zombie-proofing friendships, outsmarting creepers, protecting our skin, and other clues for faith, life, and fun!

Hey, it's go time!

60 A-to-Z Survival Secrets

This book is jam-packed with 60 survival secrets. How you use it is up to you—alone or with friends, as a daily devotional or a reference book. Share these pages with Mom and Dad or a group at church or school. Each entry includes a Minecraft adventure followed by two important sections:

Gameplay Secrets. These help you achieve success in the virtual world. Dragee90 emcees the action, defining a Minecraft A-to-Z term and offering secrets for online survival.

Real-Life Secrets. Here's where you'll find tips for success in life. Dragee90 relates the topic to the real world and shares a story, a struggle, or a victory from his own life. Each entry ends with a Bible verse, a question to think about and discuss with your friends, a faith-building step you can easily apply, and a place to jot a thought or doodle a Minecrafty masterpiece.

Escaping Aggressive Mobs

My fingers and arms are a blur of activity.

I just spawned into a brand-new game, and I don't have a second to spare. I stack block after block, trying to craft my shelter before darkness falls. Finally, the roof is attached.

Whew—that's a good start.

I race around my crude shelter, adding torches. Light is a player's best friend. I knock out some holes on each wall and fill them with blocks of glass. Eventually I'll add some cool details, like stained glass, a fancy corridor that will lead to my mine, and several more rooms—sleeping chambers, a crafting room, a big dining hall. But I can't worry about those things just yet. My number one priority is to protect myself from eminent danger.

Uh-oh, I see movement in the trees. Better hurry.

I tap into my resources and build some heavy wooden doors

to keep out the mobs. Yikes—I don't have enough weapons and food yet. I have to go back outside, but I'm losing time.

Here they come.

Moans, groans, and hissing sounds fill the air as an army of Minecraft monsters invade my world. There are fast-moving skeletons, lumbering zombies, and creepy spiders. They're definitely in attack mode. These aren't passive or neutral mobs. The creatures on my doorstep are aggressive! My best defense is shelter.

But I'm caught outside trying to gather more supplies for the night. I move as quickly as I can through the thick trees. Suddenly...creepers! They are spawning everywhere.

Quick—run!

This time my legs become a blur as I rocket home. I scream through the front door just in time and find a corner, where I hunker down for the night. (I haven't yet created a bed.)

I'm safe inside...for now.

After what seems like an eternity, nightfall covers my Minecrafty world. I peek out a window. *Yep, the freak show is in full swing!*

But something even stranger catches my eye. I can almost see my friends among the monsters outside. I imagine a neighborhood kid named Eddie dragging his feet with the zombies. (He does a pretty good imitation.) Skinny Kyle is blending in with the skeletons. And the more I look, the more I realize that Minecraft mobs are like different groups at school. My best friends are creative and nice and fun to joke around with. Some kids are passive and move right past me as if I didn't exist. There are other kids whom I don't know that well but who are good to be with when the teacher gives us team assignments.

My smile quickly fades as I think about a not-so-fun group: the mean kids.

You know the types—those who love to make fun of people... otherwise known as *bullies*. And to be honest, that's who I'm up against right now.

At school, bullies walk around in groups, acting as if they own the place. And when one turns his attention on me, the rest of them seem to want a piece of the action. They say they are just joking around and I shouldn't get upset, but their hateful words spawn like a creeper mob.

GROWL...HHHIIISSSSS...KABOOM!

That all-too familiar sound snaps me back to gameplay. I glance out the window again and cringe. The creepers are multiplying—and they're everywhere!

What else will the darkness bring?

GAMEPLAY SECRETS

Mobs (short for "mobiles") are a fact of life in Minecraft. They include villagers, animals, and monsters. They can turn otherwise peaceful gameplay into turmoil. The aggressive mobs are the worst ones. They attack players on sight, and not just when they're provoked.

But I have a survival tip that can save your life...

Dragee90's Best Tip

Monsters cannot see through glass or ice blocks. So always build windows on your shelter. This way, you can spy on them without being detected.

Read It

"There are six or seven kinds of people the LORD doesn't like: Those who are too proud or tell lies or murder, those who make evil plans or are quick to do wrong, those who tell lies in court or stir up trouble in a family" (Proverbs 6:16-19).

Think It

When you're attacked by creeper-controlled "aggressive mobs," do you stop and think before you speak? Or do you push back with anger, fueling the fire? Do you pray? How would Jesus want you to react?

Live It

There will always be mean people in the world. And since we can't always avoid them, it's a good idea to have a plan for when they attack. The best defense is to know that we are wonderfully and creatively made by God. We have a special set of skills that God wants to use to make the world a better place. Our identity is not decided by a few jerks who are just trying to look cool in front of others. So take a deep breath and resist fighting back in the same hurtful ways. Instead, find shelter. God has our back, and He has given us *real* friends. Step back and look at the troublemakers through the glass window. You'll quickly see their actions in a new light.

Putting on Your Protective **Armor**

Go, go, go...and then *jump!*

Downward I fly until I land safely on the glass ceiling of my dome. I don't see any danger, but I know it's just around the corner. I may as well go into the woods to see what adventures this world has to offer.

I race through the trees, dodging branches, cliffs, and the occasional animal. I move toward a warm orange glow just beyond the trees. Suddenly, I'm on the edge of flowing lava.

I can't go left, I can't go right, but I might be able to make it through the narrow passage straight ahead. It's decision time. *Never mind!* I play it smart and decide it's time to shop. So into the villager trader I go.

Sometimes we can just feel the danger ahead. It can be a group of kids who gather in the hallway at school. You know the kind—they find strength in numbers and make fun of people as they walk by. Or maybe it's a grumpy old man who likes to let his barking dogs out into the yard every time someone passes by. Or even an older sibling who is annoyed by your every move.

These everyday dangers aren't always avoidable. There are times when we have to just walk straight through them. It's a good thing we have real-life armor to wear. I'm not talking about the heavy knights-in-shining-armor kind of gear that brave warriors strapped on long, long ago. I'm talking about the armor of God. God has given us armor that helps us do more than just survive. He has given us *truth*, *righteousness*, *justice*, *peace*, *faith*, and *His Spirit*. Best of all, it's free. We don't have to save up, purchase it, or even earn it. It's just a bonus of being a child of God. All we have to do is grab it, wear it, and walk through life's lava pits with confidence.

Back in the game, I notice that I have a lot of iron units to tap into as I trade for some armor. I choose boots, a helmet, and some trousers. Done. I jump back into the game and check my armor durability in the corner of my screen.

It's time to run for my life. I lean forward and run on the middle path right through the lava. For a moment, I can't even see what my next step holds. But I push through.

Wow...those trousers and boots saved me. There's no way I could have made it past that lava pit without them.

I check my armor level again, and I still have a lot of defensive points left.

Leather, gold, chain mail, iron, and diamond—each of these elements can be crafted into a player's all-important armor. And wearing this kind of protection is essential for survival, especially in PVP (player versus player).

Dragee90's Best Tip

I like to create my armor out of diamonds. They provide the greatest defense against attack, but they're also the hardest to acquire. Also, *always* wear your armor (and bring a torch) when you head into a dark place, such as a mine.

REAL-LIFE SECRETS

Read It

"Be ready! Let the truth be like a belt around your waist, and let God's justice protect you like armor. Your desire to tell the good news about peace should be like shoes on your feet. Let your faith be like a shield, and you will be able to stop all the flaming arrows of the evil one. Let God's saving power be like a helmet, and for a sword use God's message that comes from the Spirit" (Ephesians 6:14-17).

Think It

Are you wearing the armor of God? Exactly what is it? (Look at the verses above and identify each piece.)

Live It

I'd never face a hostile Minecraft mob without my armor...and it's the same way in real life.
So just as today's Bible passage instructs, I put on
my spiritual armor:

The belt of truth and the Bible, our sword. The better my
grasp of Scripture, the bigger my belt buckle. So I
read God's Word.

The gospel of peace, our combat boots. If we're not wearing our combat boots, it's like we're walking on
thorny ground in bare feet. It's a good idea to put
them on before leaving the house. How? Connect
with Jesus through prayer and share your faith
through your very life—being kind and loving to
others.

The shield of faith. Jesus is our shield (Psalm 84:11)
and the source of our faith (Galatians 2:20). He protects us from the flaming arrows of the evil one.

The helmet of salvation. Salvation is all about a thrilling life with Jesus, which is His gift to us (John
10:10). Every minute we're enjoying that excitement,
our helmet is on. And with that helmet firmly in
place, our minds are guarded from Satan's lies.

Firing an **A**rrow with Pinpoint Accuracy

H ere comes a creeper.

I duck behind a tree before running first to my right and then to my left. I zigzag through the jungle. *Oh no, there's another one.*

It seems like everywhere I turn, creepers pop out of nowhere and begin attacking me.

At first sight, they look harmless—but definitely weird. They have swampy, greenish-black bodies and clawlike feet. Their ghoulish eyes lock on to their prey. And even though they don't have arms, creepers can climb ropes and ladders with ease. They can jump really far too.

Here's what drives me crazy: They are virtually silent. This makes it hard to detect them. But if you get too close, you'll hear a very distinct *HIIISSS...SIZZZZLE.* At that point, run...because the very next sound will be *KABOOM!*

Creepers destroy everything in their path.

I go for my favorite weapon—my arrow. This handy tool is made from sticks, flints, and feathers, and it flies through the air with ease. It also keeps me at a safe distance from the creepers.

I love shooting a bow in real life. It's one of my favorite activities at summer camp! And I've learned that this weapon has been around for a long time. Before modern discoveries, people used bows and arrows for hunting and survival. In the Bible, Zechariah even describes the Lord using them in his defense. That's pretty cool.

WHOOSH!

I spot a creeper in my path, so I take aim and let an arrow fly.

My first shot sticks in a tree. My second disappears into the air. This is dangerous. If it falls down on my own head, I could injure myself. (Yep, even in Minecraft.)

The moment is tense, but I manage to keep my cool. In spite of the losses, I know my arrows will never fail me. What they symbolize gives me confidence.

For me, an arrow is a reminder that God is my protector. The Lord defended His people with arrows in the Old Testament, and He's still protecting each one of us in different ways—just as He protected my friends and me one day when we were climbing around on some rocks in Colorado and got lost. All of a sudden, we didn't know which way to go. I immediately began to pray, "Dear God, help us. It's scary out here, and we don't even have any water with us. Please help us find our way."

We started out on a path but soon found ourselves in the middle of a field with a bunch of cows. We were lost. My friends began to pray out loud. Suddenly, we saw a road. We made our way to the pavement, followed the signs, and were soon back with our parents. They were happy and upset at the same time. But I knew that God had protected us out there. He gave us the strength and wisdom to keep moving forward. Prayer was my tool that day. God worked through it to protect me.

And at this very moment, my trusty bow and arrow are the right tools.

I weave left and right to a place in the woods that has more sunlight. Now I can see the ghoulish green guys more clearly, so I let my arrows fly. I take four creepers down before heading back to my shelter. And I'd better hurry—it's getting dark, and the creepers will begin to spawn at a crazy rate.

There's never a dull moment in Minecraft.

Come to think of it, that describes life in the real world too!

GAMEPLAY SECRETS

Knowing how to use a bow and arrow is a key to thriving, not just surviving, in Minecraft. They are tools used for hunting, not to mention safeguards against zombies, creepers, and other mobs. But players have to make each shot count. If you react quickly and strike a target with pinpoint accuracy, you can rack up *hit points* and save your life.

Dragee90's Best Tip

Pull the arrow all the way back before firing it. This enables the arrow to go farther and causes the most damage.

Read It

"The Lord will appear above his people; his arrows will fly like lightning! The Sovereign Lord will sound the ram's horn and attack like a whirlwind from the southern desert" (Zechariah 9:14 NLT).

Think It

Do you run to God when you are in trouble? Do you call out to Him for protection, or do you try to rely on your own abilities?

Live It

Practice helps. If you regularly pray and read your Bible, this interaction with God becomes a part of your life. Then when you need help or guidance, you can more easily begin to pray to seek the Scriptures for wisdom. You can always do these things, even if you're out of practice. But why wait? Get started today by having a chat with God. He will be happy to hear from you.

**Jot a Thought or Dream Up
a Minecrafty Masterpiece**

Ultimate Attack Strategies

Oh no, they're coming from every direction!

O   I spin, jump, and swing. But I'm just too out-numbered. I know the mobs have won as my skin begins to flash and eventually disappear from the screen. Suddenly I find myself back where I first spawned into this world.

One basic mistake, and now I have to start over again. I know what I did wrong—I ventured too far away from my shelter. I'd spent so much time and a ton of resources creating the best shelter ever. It was full of supplies, food, and weapons to keep me safe through the night. Even though daytime lasts only ten minutes in this world, I was caught up in exploring and didn't get back in time. Rookie mistake. And now I've realized that I've made another rookie mistake. I didn't mark my way from my spawn point to my shelter.

How am I going to get back?

I know better. I know that the best strategies for an attack begin with my defense. But building a strong shelter can work for me only if I put it to use as I am taking on creepers, dodging explosions, or running from falling anvils. A good base camp with a 360-degree view, is best positioned in a place where I can turn the tables on my attackers and make them run into the woods to get away from me. If I venture out on short trips in all directions—always keeping my shelter within reach—I can gather information on the enemy's strongholds. If I get in trouble, I can always retreat to the safety of my shelter. And if I build a tall beacon with a torch on top, I'll be able to locate it in the middle of an attack.

It's just like real life. You have to build up a strong shelter. A place that is safe, full of food, stockpiled with resources, and easy to find in the dark. Fortunately, you always have shelter in God. He is with you whether you're at home, in school, or on your bike. This kind of knowledge is helpful in any crazy situation you may find yourself in. It will bring you peace as you learn about your world and practice moving through it strategically.

Gathering information and having options will lead to success as I navigate this world. How else would I learn that the best way to kill a spider is to make it fall off of a cliff? Or that silverfish will sink if you lead them into soul sand? Yep, knowledge is key.

GAMEPLAY SECRETS

Many kids enjoy multiplayer. And they can't get enough of the Minecraft version of *Hunger Games*—sort of a virtual paintball battle with an army of strange creatures and other players coming at them from every direction. So in the heat of battle, they need a winning edge—strategies that separate the *noobs* from the pros.

Dragee90's Best Tip

Here's a tactic I use when the enemy is coming at me: I shield and then hit rapidly. This enables you to block and hit at the same time, so you'll end up receiving half the damage while inflicting normal damage. This trick can help you survive another day.

REAL-LIFE SECRETS

Read It

"We show our love for God by obeying his commandments, and they are not hard to follow. Every child of God can defeat the world, and our faith is what gives us this victory. No one can defeat the world without having faith in Jesus as the Son of God" (1 John 5:3-5).

Think It

Why is it important to obey God's commandments? What gives us victory in the world? (Please explain.)

Live It

Our heart and our mouth—these are the two main centers of obedience to God. That's why David prayed, "May these words of my mouth and this meditation of my heart be pleasing in your sight, LORD, my Rock and my Redeemer" (Psalm 19:14 NIV). He knew that if he could just let his heavenly Father take control of his heart and his mouth, he could live a holy life—a life that would be a great witness to God's glory and grace. That's how I want to live. How about you?

Jot a Thought or Dream Up a Minecrafty Masterpiece

Building on
Bedrock

I swing my axe as I dig deeper and deeper into the ground below.

I have plenty of coal, iron, and gold. And I love my obsidian and granite. But now I need more bedrock. It's not fancy, and it can't make armor, create circuits, or be used as payments for other items. But it's solid and the best material to fortify my shelter.

Fortunately, bedrock is everywhere. It can be found in the bottom layers of the Overworld and in the Nether. And it's easy to find because it always generates in the same pattern regardless of the seed used. But it can't be mined with a pickaxe like the other minerals. So I'm taking a break from the action, and I'm spending a little time in creative inventory mode so I can stockpile some bedrock. I head to the surface and use the downloaded mod called Single Player Commands. I hit the *T* and open the command line. I input *give* and the number 07, which is the code for bedrock.

Now I have bedrock in my inventory.

This common mineral can withstand creepers who attack in the night. It cannot be broken by tools, and it can't be destroyed by explosions. It's the only block that a beacon beam can shine through at night. And it's one of the materials used to create an End gateway portal when the ender dragon is killed.

We need bedrocks in our lives. They're solid pieces that go unnoticed but are so important in life—having a strong faith, a safe home, and a family that loves us. These are the building blocks that give us shelter when we are attacked or scared, or when we don't know what's going on. It's important to gather these things together and rely on them every day. Grow in your knowledge about your faith. Protect your family members as they protect you. Find shelter in the storm as you hold onto the bedrocks in your life. They are beacons you can always find in the middle of the night.

I wonder what this world would be like if there were no bedrock? If all of the minerals I found were shiny or beautiful? Or if building materials were too hard to mine, and I was left without a strong shelter? I surely wouldn't make it through the night.

GAMEPLAY SECRETS

It's indestructible. You can't break through bedrock with a pickaxe, and even an explosion can't scratch it. So what's the point of it? It serves as a foundation.

Dragee90's Best Tip

When you reach the End in the game for the final battle, set some bedrock on fire. The flame will never go out and will light your way. And here's another neat trick about bedrock (something most players don't think about): When you spawn in the End, you'll end up on a platform of bedrock. Stay by the platform so you can be shielded from the ender dragon's fire blasts.

REAL-LIFE SECRETS

Read It

"Anyone who hears and obeys these teachings of mine is like a wise person who built a house on solid rock. Rain poured down, rivers flooded, and winds beat against that house. But it did not fall, because it was built on solid rock" (Matthew 7:24-25).

Think It

What is the solid rock? How do we build our lives on it?

Live It

Too many of my friends are brainwashed by lies from magazines, movies, TV, and peers at school. The biggest lie they're swallowing goes something like this: "Whatever! If it works for you, then that's your truth. What's right for one person may be wrong for his neighbor." In other words, they are buying the lie that everything is okay—any god, any set of rules, any sense of right and wrong, and any thoughts of the afterlife are all different for each individual. Look closely, and you begin to see that this way of thinking is full of holes.

There is only one rock-solid truth—one bedrock. Truth comes from God. Where can we build on it? As we saw in the verse above, we build on solid rock by following the teachings of Jesus in the Bible.

Jot a Thought or Dream Up a Minecrafty Masterpiece

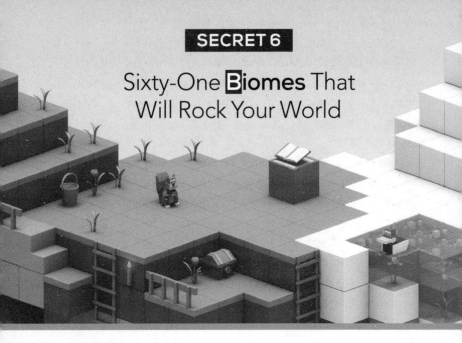

Sixty-One Biomes That Will Rock Your World

Jungle M—that's my world. And during our tour earlier, you saw firsthand why it's so special. It has the perfect 95-degree weather mixed with so many plants, flowers, and vines that it's hard to see the sky. The ground is covered, and the trees are so tall they poke through the clouds. It's definitely the most demanding terrain, but it rewards its inhabitants with an abundance of resources.

The possibilities are endless here! I can mine, craft, and explore to my heart's content. But I can't ever let down my guard. Along with abundance comes challenge. Dark threats hide in paradise.

Forest, jungle, grassland, desert, ice plains, ocean, extreme hills—these are the basic Minecraft landscapes (or *biomes*). Biomes are split into five categories based on their temperature: snow-covered, cold, medium, dry/warm, and neutral.

It's cool how the different worlds in Minecraft remind me

of some place on earth. From the desert sands to the snow-packed mountains, it's all based on the different regions of the real world. The mesa biomes remind me of our family vacation to Arizona. The ocean biomes look like the sea view from a cruise ship. The swamplands have lily pads just like the Okefenokee Swamp in Florida.

I have a lot of fun creating within the different biomes in Minecraft. But even with all of my creativity flowing, it doesn't even begin to compare to our amazing world. The more I learn about how the earth, plants, animals, and people need each other to survive, the more I'm blown away. God created this detailed world with the perfect gravity, food, and warmth needed to sustain life. His creativity continues to fascinate me.

Ever read the creation account in the Bible? Sometime soon, flip open your Bible to Genesis 1 and read the chapter. Here's a very special story based on that passage.

God speaks. Darkness hides. A soup of nothingness suddenly bursts with light and color and warmth.

God creates—water, air, sky, earth. And living beings!

Creatures spring forth in every size and shape, splashing through the seas and thundering across the plains. Chirping. Flapping. Swarming. Bleating. Gnawing. Clawing. Digging.

"It is good."

God gives. His essence. His heart. Himself.

As He reaches into the ground, dust pours through His fingers. But then He begins to form it, molding sand and mud into something familiar. A foot. An arm. A face. His greatest masterpiece.

"Let us make human beings in our image, make them reflecting our nature so they can be responsible for the fish in the sea, the birds in the air, the cattle, and, yes, Earth itself, and every animal that moves on the face of the Earth."*

God animates. Lungs inflate. Hearts beat. Eyes open wide—gazing back into His.

Humans: spirit, flesh, reason, emotion, passion, creativity, intellect. The finest reflection of God that He could dream up. His image. His family. Adam and Eve.

God blesses. And the first man and woman rule over the Earth.

"Prosper! Reproduce! Fill the Earth! Take charge! Be responsible for fish in the sea and birds in the air, for every living thing that moves on the face of Earth."†

God rests. The world is complete. His work is finished.

"It is good, so very good."

I've spawned into other biomes, and I've determined that I'm a jungle boy through and through. The stone beach biomes and Extreme Hills M biome are too rocky and gray. The Ice Plains Spikes biome looks cool, but it has limited green plants. Mushroom island biomes are interesting with their nightly mob attacks and naturally spawning 'shrooms. The cacti are fun in the desert biomes, but there aren't very many things to hide behind.

Of all the Minecraft worlds I've explored, I prefer Jungle M.

---

* Genesis 1:26 MSG

† Genesis 1:28 MSG

GAMEPLAY SECRETS

Did you know that there are 61 distinct landscapes in Minecraft? This is what makes the game so fun. Some are cold and some are hot; some are filled with jungles and mountains, and others are empty. But each one is filled with secrets to discover.

Dragee90's Best Tip

On your first day in the game, you'll suddenly appear—or *spawn*—in a randomly generated environment. It begins at the crack of dawn, but there isn't a moment to waste. (A day in Minecraft lasts only ten minutes in real life.) So what should you do first? Here's what I suggest: Gather resources and build a shelter. Look for any useful item—trees, rocks, cactus—and start building walls and a roof...and especially a barrier around your makeshift house. Hit the trunk of a tree repeatedly with your hand, and a section will fall away as a cube of wood. You can add this to your inventory. Do the same with rocks and cacti. Each of these resources can be used as you build a shelter.

REAL-LIFE SECRETS

Read It

"You alone are the LORD, Creator of the heavens and all the stars, Creator of the earth and those who live on it, Creator of the ocean and all its creatures. You are the source of life, praised by the stars that fill the heavens" (Nehemiah 9:6).

Think It

When you discover something new about our world, do you stop and think about how creative God is?

Live It

When you learn about molecules in science class, be impressed with how God built our world—from the smallest part to the larger picture. When you recover from being sick, think about how amazing the human body is, designed to heal itself. When the leaves begin to change color in the fall, remember how God has designed the earth to have seasons and cycles. You can find God's creativity everywhere. And He wants us to be a part of it as we live our lives. When thinking about our Creator, remember Nehemiah 9:6, which says, "You alone are the Lord."

Jot a Thought or Dream Up a Minecrafty Masterpiece

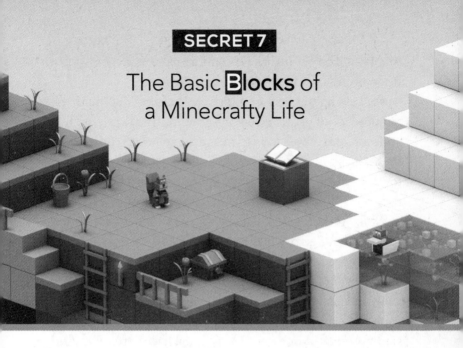

The Basic Blocks of a Minecrafty Life

I'm taking a little trip to build up my inventory.

I hope to find diamonds, sponges, diorite, and sandstone. As I travel across the Overworld, I discover some unusual blocks along the surface. But I'm missing some tools that would allow me to grab them. And I'm definitely not equipped to dig for most of them.

I have my axe, but I'm missing a pickaxe and a shovel. How frustrating. I grab two sticks and three units of wood planks and craft a pickaxe. Yet that's not good enough because it only has a durability of 60. I need a stronger one. So I go to work again by grabbing two more sticks and three iron units, and that increases the durability to 251. Of course, it's just easier to get a pickaxe from a bonus chest. Unfortunately, I need one now.

A wooden pickaxe can mine most ores, but I'm going to need the iron one if I'm lucky enough to find some gold ore.

And I'll still be out of luck if I come across a block of obsidian. It can be mined only with a diamond pickaxe.

As I swing my new iron pickaxe, I discover so many different kinds of blocks below the ground. There's clay, granite, andesite, and gravel. My pickaxe turns green as I come across these blocks, indicating they can be mined with my trusty iron tool. But of course, it turns red as I come across layers of bedrock. Why? They can't be mined this way.

Still, I'm feeling really lucky today as I hit the F3 button and see that I've reached elevation Y = 10. Now I'm on the hunt for the rare minerals of gold, redstone, diamond, and emerald. Of course, I'm going to have to obtain a better pickaxe if I plan on mining diamond. The Y tells me how deep I've gone, the X determines east from west, and Z is for north and south. And everyone knows that you'll have better luck finding these rare ores between Y = 10 and Y = 5.

I would have missed out on so many useful minerals if I had stayed on the surface. It would have been easier but not nearly as productive. We have so many more options in real life when we dig deep, work hard, and gather as many resources as we can. We grow in our faith when we take the time to read our Bibles. We discover new words and ideas as we study what we read. Our hearts are filled with peace when we take time to pray. And we find new friends when we invest in the lives of those around us. It takes some practice, and sometimes we have to learn some new skills. But it helps us to shape a far better world.

GAMEPLAY SECRETS

Blocks are what Minecraft is all about, and there are dozens and dozens of them: air, water, fire, dirt, leather, wool, diamond, gold...the list seems endless. Everything is created and built out of these tiny cubes. And the worlds kids create are amazing. You can craft anything with Minecraft blocks: a castle, a cruise ship, a Martian city, the Mona Lisa. No kidding!

Dragee90's Best Tip

Here's what every serious player must build: In survival mode, create a shelter and a farm. In creative mode, construct a castle and a city.

REAL-LIFE SECRETS

Read It

"The LORD God took a handful of soil and made a man. God breathed life into the man, and the man started breathing. The LORD made a garden in a place called Eden, which was in the east, and he put the man there" (Genesis 2:7-8).

Think It

When the Bible refers to God as our Creator, what does that mean? How does it make you feel, knowing that you are a one-of-a-kind, unique individual who was created by God? (Please explain.)

Live It

The fingerprints of God are everywhere—even on *you*. Your body, for example, is a marvelously created and complex machine. At school, I'm learning that inside our bodies are cells that build themselves from carefully designed and coded information—instructions that have been passed from one life to the next since their original inception. Study your hands. Together, they have one-fourth of all the bones in your body. With them, you can create the most delicate painting or lift heavy weights. And your very own fingerprints are uniquely yours. Mind-boggling! Yet here's something that's even better: God knows you, loves you, and has numbered every hair on the top of your head! (See Luke 12:7.) Our lives matter to the Lord—so be confident!

Jot a Thought or Dream Up a Minecrafty Masterpiece

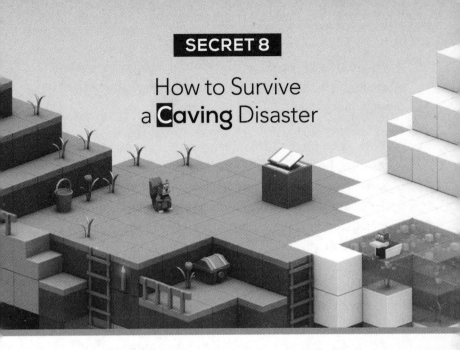

How to Survive a **C**aving Disaster

Deep. Dark. Dangerous.

It's the eerie, alien world of a Minecraft cave. My heart pounds as I click my mouse and descend into the blackness with nothing but a pickaxe and a torch. I'm in survival mode, so I know what's ahead: spiders, skeletons, zombies, creepers. But I selected the *normal* setting, which means I can handle whatever trouble comes my way. Now, if I'd tapped on *hardcore* mode, it would be game over!

I'm on a mission today. My weapons arsenal is pretty weak—just a bow and arrow and a broken stone sword. That's pretty sad, so it's time to upgrade...and I have my eye on the ultimate defensive tool—a bluish-green, super-durable diamond sword. I know exactly where to find one. A villager has agreed to part with one in exchange for three emeralds. I'm thrilled! But there's just one tiny, little snag with my big plan: I don't have a single emerald! Even worse, they're hard to find.

So I'm trekking deep into the abyss of a large cavern some-where in the hill country—desperately hoping to unearth the precious blocks I need.

TAP, TAP, TAP...POP!

With just a torch to see by, I dig my pickaxe into the walls. No luck yet, but the caves in this biome are known for hiding massive deposits of every type of ore. And I just passed an underground lake, not to mention a river of lava...so I must be headed in the right direction. In fact, I have a really good feeling about this mission. (Famous last words, right?)

As I mine the gems, I can't help thinking about the caves I've explored in the real world. There are plenty not far from my home in Missouri, which I bet were places that inspired Mark Twain. (Have you ever read his adventures about Tom Sawyer and Huckleberry Finn?) But my favorite cave is in Colorado. It's filled with stalactites and stalagmites; twisting, narrow passageways; large, open chambers with pools of water; and...*gulp*...spiders. Yuck! I hate spiders! I'd never dare set foot in that place without a headlamp, a compass, and a professional guide to steer me away from danger and to watch over every step I took. It's the same in life. I'd never think of stepping out my front door without the Lord's guidance and protection.

Suddenly...*yikes!*

I come face-to-face with glowing red eyes! It's a massive spider, and it's ready to pounce. (Yep, I spoke too soon!) I wave my torch and swing my pickaxe. I miss the creature but strike the cave wall. And right before my eyes...*BOOM!* The exposed blocks light up. "I've struck the mother lode," I yell.

Seams of diamonds and emeralds sparkle before me. The spider disappears into the darkness. Mission complete! I pack up the diamonds and emeralds and begin my journey out of this strange, subterranean place. It's time to meet a certain villager and get my diamond sword.

GAMEPLAY SECRETS

This is where Indiana Jones meets Minecraft. Exploring a cave can get your heart pounding because you never know what you'll encounter—hidden treasure or monster trouble? Some caves have tunnels that branch off and wind in multiple directions; some have narrow tunnels that lead to dark dead ends. And every cavern has an element of danger.

Dragee90's Best Tip

Whenever I enter a cave, I don't start mining right away. Instead, I head to the end of a tunnel, torch it up, and then mine the rock on my way out. This ensures that fewer monsters spawn as I find precious resources—and it helps me avoid disaster.

REAL-LIFE SECRETS

Read It

"With all your heart you must trust the LORD and not your own judgment" (Proverbs 3:5).

Think It

Why is it important to trust the Lord with all our heart? In what ways can our own judgment fail us?

Live It

My dad and I love to go caving in Missouri and backpacking in Colorado. And the best part of our wilderness adventures? Sitting by a crackling campfire, roasting marshmallows, making s'mores, and just talking. But the second I step away from the warm fire, the world becomes a dark, scary place. Just making my way to the tent can be a challenge. That's when I click on my trusty flashlight. It guides my steps and keeps me from falling on my face or getting lost in the woods.

Guess what? My faith in Jesus guides my path in life. His Word (the Bible), prayer, and the godly teaching I get from my parents and my church help me to know Jesus better. As my pastor says, "Jesus is the answer to everything, the One who guides us from darkness to life!"

Jot a Thought or Dream Up a Minecrafty Masterpiece

SECRET 9

What to Hide in Your Chest

I've named my shelter Mount Quack, and it has taken me hours to build—block by block, room by room. It's my own royal hideaway, sort of a medieval-styled, Irish-Scandinavian chateau that honors my heritage. (Flip back to "Starting Point" for detailed descriptions.)

Little by little, I'm filling each room with chests—from small to large. Most are practical and hold everyday stuff: weapons, tools, and food. But others would turn the most ruthless scallywag of a pirate into a Minecraft believer. I've packed my favorite chests with rare treasure: emeralds, gold, and diamonds. Emeralds are like the game's version of currency. I trade these with villagers for things I need. Gold and diamonds are used for weapons and armor. But regardless of the item, each thing I've made or acquired has a special place...and that place usually involves a chest.

I wish my real-life hideaway (my bedroom) looked like my

Minecraft shelter. Imagine a place created out of giant rock blocks with torches lining the walls, stained-glass windows, and passageways that lead to tall towers and deep mines. And picture wooden chests tucked away in corners, each one hiding cool stuff: tools, treasure...secrets that protect me from the enemy. My real-life room is pretty good at hiding things too—remote controls, overdue library books, socks that match. Unfortunately, my little piece of the world is...uh, well...maybe a *little* messy. (Okay, a lot messy.) But thankfully, I carry with me answers that guide me through this messy world—truth that's hidden deep in my heart. I'm talking, of course, about God's Word.

I keep Scripture on the tip of my tongue and carry it everywhere I go—even into my Minecrafty world. When I'm mining or crafting or talking to other players, God is right there.

Remember Lenny, my ocelot-turned-cuddly cat? I learned the hard way that if he's standing above a chest, it won't open. No kidding!

A skeleton was coming toward my window, and I had to act fast. "Time to pull out my trusty bow and arrow," I told Lenny. But when I tried to open my chest filled with weapons, it seemed to be stuck.

"What's goin' on?" I yelled. I looked at Lenny, and the cat just blinked. And then he hopped off his perch and tiptoed out of the room with his usual proud, stealthy stride.

Seconds afterward, the chest magically opened.

"Aha!" I exclaimed. "Note to self: A chest plus an ocelot equals an extra security measure. That just might come in handy."

GAMEPLAY SECRETS

Oak, spruce, birch, acacia, jungle...the choice of wood is up to you. But once you've gathered eight planks, you're on your way to creating a customized storage area that can't be moved, burned, destroyed by lava, or raided by strangers. Chests come in two sizes, large and small, and they're perfect for keeping valuable items safe. What kinds of things?

Dragee90's Best Tip

I put food, tools, and my sword in my chest—items I need to stay alive in the game. And there are a few essential secrets I always place in my chest: diamonds and emeralds. This keeps them safe—and it makes me feel like a pirate!

REAL-LIFE SECRETS

Read It

"I treasure your word above all else; it keeps me from sinning against you" (Psalm 119:11).

Think It

Why do you think God's Word is able to keep us from sinning? Why is it important to study and know Scripture?

Live It

What's inside that big, thick book with very few pictures and lots and lots of words? I'm talking, of course, about the Bible. It's important that we find out because God's words are the most important words we'll ever read. When we allow His message to become ours, we invite His life to surge through us. And through the verses and lessons we will find inside, we'll get to know Jesus better—to walk with Him, to become like Him...to have a deeper relationship with Him. The Scriptures help us to do this. And it's important to hide God's Word in our hearts. In other words, we need to commit Scripture to memory.

Jot a Thought or Dream Up a Minecrafty Masterpiece

Coal—a Minecrafter's Prized Resource

I look at my furnace and cringe. "Pathetic," I tell myself.

My fuel supply is getting low, and I have a lot of work ahead—cooking, smelting, and creating cool stuff. Time to get some coal.

A short time later, I strap on my diamond armor and grab my pickaxe, my diamond sword, and my favorite weapon—my bow. (I'm a good shot, and my bow has always helped me ward off subterranean mobs.) Before I know it, I'm descending into the deep, narrow shaft that drops into my mine. A wooden ladder is the only way down. Dozens and dozens of torches light my way.

My mine is rich with elements, especially the rare kind, like diamond ore. And abundant veins of coal stretch to a range of more than 50 blocks. My biggest deposits are found between elevations $Y = 4$ and $Y = 31$. (Remember, the lowest bedrock layer is $Y = 0$, and sea level is $Y = 64$.) I get busy at elevation $Y = 10$.

SMACK! WACK! BAM!

My pickaxe exposes the beautiful gray-and-black-speckled blocks I've come for. It's a Minecrafter's prized resource. But as with anything worthwhile, getting it involves challenge.

WACK! WACK! WACK!

As I strike the blocks, I accidently hit a monster egg—which is identical to all the other blocks. *Hmmm...this one's stubborn,* I tell myself—not realizing what I've uncovered. I pound it over and over. Big mistake.

A hostile, buglike creature—a silverfish—awakens and attacks me. Without thinking, I pull out my bow and unleash a swarm of arrows. That makes matters worse! Other silverfish appear from nowhere and join the attack.

"My sword!" I scream. So I grab it and let the weapon fly. My quick thinking pays off. The silverfish retreat, and I'm safe once again.

It's time to collect my prize and return to my Minecrafty mission.

In the real world, miners sacrifice so much to find coal. They gather it out of loyalty—commitment to their families, communities, and friends. They do it to earn a paycheck and to carve out a life above the ground. My grandpa Floyd was one of those brave people. He spent his entire life taking care of those he loved. And through his life, he pointed the way to the greatest treasure of all—eternity with Jesus Christ.

Back at Mount Quack, my grandpa's memory races through my mind as I stoke the coal and fuel my Minecraft furnace. *He spent his life mining true treasure,* I remind myself. *He found his purpose leading others to God. And that's got to be my mission too.*

Coal is obtained by mining coal ore with a pickaxe and is most commonly used as fuel for heat, cooking, and smelting in a furnace. It's also great to trade for other necessary items. For example, villager fishermen, armorers, and tool smiths buy 16 to 24 coal blocks for one precious emerald block. Coal is valuable in Minecraft.

Dragee90's Best Tip

Coal is a source of light—which is important at night when the monsters come out. I use it to make torches that surround my shelter, and of course it fuels my furnace. Wood is fine, but coal works better.

REAL-LIFE SECRETS

Read It

"Each of you has been blessed with one of God's many wonderful gifts to be used in the service of others. So use your gift well. If you have the gift of speaking, preach God's message. If you have the gift of helping others, do it with the strength that God supplies. Everything should be done in a way that will bring honor to God because of Jesus Christ, who is glorious and powerful forever. Amen" (1 Peter 4:10-11).

Think It

What are some of the gifts (abilities) that God has blessed you with? How can you use those gifts to serve Jesus?

Live It

My grandpa Floyd mined coal in the tiny West Virginia town of Pineville. "Coal is valuable, but it's not the *real* treasure in life," he used to tell everybody. He'd say this to everyone from burly miners to the busloads of kids he would drive to church on Sunday mornings. "It's not even nearly the most valuable." Then he'd hold up his Bible. "This is the true treasure." My grandpa was a miner and a preacher...and most important, a strong man of God. He used his gifts to serve others and to help them know Jesus. That's how I want to use my gifts too.

Jot a Thought or Dream Up a Minecrafty Masterpiece

Crafting
with Purpose

I't's amazing what people dream up and create in Minecraft.

I've seen a floating "aqua base" with boats and aircraft; twisting, looping roller coasters; a realistic cruise ship like the one my family and I sailed on to the Bahamas; castles so real I'm convinced I read about them in a history lesson. And my favorite creation? It's a giant basketball arena with multiple courts, locker rooms, and a snack shop. I could actually play a game there—jumping around a court, shooting balls, and blocking shots. Incredible!

Today, I'm working on Mount Quack—my medieval-styled, Irish-Scandinavian chateau. I'm adding an indoor swimming pool with a glass ceiling to let in tons of light. One end of the giant space will have a mini golf course, and the other side will have a garden filled with trees and bright, tropical plants. *Hmm*...maybe I'll throw in a basketball court too. Why not? It's our Minecrafty world, and there's no limit to our imaginations!

I wish doing homework could be this fun. I have to admit, sometimes I expend minimal effort at school. Sometimes my handwriting is sloppy, and I throw together a project at the last minute just to get it done. I'm not proud to admit this—just being honest. My mom says that if I'd use the same imagination with my lessons as I do with Minecraft, I'd be a much better student. Don't tell her I said this, but she's right!

Back in the game, I move a glass block from my inventory and place it in one of the hotkey slots on my screen. This allows me to assign the block. *TAP, TAP, TAP.* When I select that specific slot, the block appears in my hand, ready to be placed exactly where I want it.

Yep, I'm crafting with purpose, and it's paying off. Mount Quack is really shaping up. Mom will be proud. And it's time to be this creative in the real world too.

GAMEPLAY SECRETS

A big part of Minecraft is crafting—building stuff with virtual, Lego-like blocks. (Hey, the word *craft* is part of the name!) This is what helps players survive and thrive...and create amazing worlds. Every item is crafted using raw materials—wood, stone, and diamond ore, for example. The crafting grid is a 2x2 in inventory or a 3x3 crafting table, which is where the Minecraft magic happens.

Dragee90's Best Tip

Let your imagination run wild! (This is my favorite part of the game.) You pull items from your inventory and move them into your crafting grid or table—using the right amounts and arranging them in the correct pattern—and...*POW!* You just crafted something.

Read It

"Do your work willingly, as though you were serving the Lord himself, and not just your earthly master. In fact, the Lord Christ is the one you are really serving, and you know that he will reward you" (Colossians 3:23-24).

Think It

Do you sometimes get upset when your parents stop the fun and make you do chores? (Please explain.) What kind of attitude does God want you to have?

Live It

"Take out the trash and then clean your room," my mom often tells me. Sometimes I grumble. Sometimes I just don't want to do it. I'd rather shoot hoops with a friend or be on my computer playing, well, my favorite game—Minecraft! But then my dad reminds me about what the Bible says: "Do your work willingly, as though you were serving the Lord himself." I can't argue with that. God wants us to have a good attitude when we do chores or homework, or are taking part in a service project at church. "The Lord Christ is the one you are really serving."

Outsmarting Creepers

Not now!" I shout.

I'm underground exploring one of my mine's deepest, darkest shafts, standing face-to-snout with a nasty green ghoul. It's the hostile mob I dread the most—a creeper!

"Lenny, I sure wish you could get me out of this jam...*again!*"

My cat companion usually manages to protect me from these guys, but not today. I'm all alone, and the only thing I can do right now is act like Indiana and *run!*

"*Yeeeooowwweee!*"

I race as fast as my duck legs will take me—bouncing, hopping, and literally flying at times. I glance over my shoulder and gasp. "The creepy creeper is gaining on me!"

And then I hear that sickening warning: *HHHIIISSSSS.* "It's gonna blow!"

KABOOM!

I escape the blast and dive into a roomy cavern. But my circumstances go from bad to worse. Now I'm surrounded by an angry gang of creepers.

"Lava," I mumble. "That's it."

Just ahead is an orange flow of glowing lava right next to a big pool of water. So I fake right and then twist my body left, pulling off a perfect parkour move. I vault off the side of the cave wall, somersault over the lava, and plunge beak-first into the water.

In a mad frenzy, the creepers collide into each other, and like dominos, they tumble one by one into molten muck.

I lean back and float on the water. A big grin slowly stretches across my face. "I love being a ninja duck—especially when I'm able to outsmart a creeper."

Isn't it crazy how joy can turn to panic in a split second? That's just a fact of life in Minecraft...and in the real world. I'll never forget a creeper encounter I had one day at school. My friends and I were having fun shooting hoops when another kid stepped on the court and took the ball. He then started shoving my buddies when they tried to get it back. My solution: Invite him to play basketball too. It worked.

Back in the cave, my soothing float is interrupted by howls and moans echoing through the tunnel. "It's not safe here," I remind myself. So it's time for another smart move—returning to the protection of my shelter.

Creepers are particularly vicious mobs that are aggressive toward players. They make sharp *HISSSSS* sounds just before they explode, so it's important to use caution when fighting them.

Dragee90's Best Tip

I can't stand these mobs. They run toward you and explode, attempting to destroy everything in sight. But here's how you can outsmart these annoying creatures: Follow what I call my "hit/run, hit/run" strategy. In other words, hit a creeper with your sword and then run to safety. Hit it again and retreat once more. Do this over and over until...*ZAP*...it just disappears.

REAL-LIFE SECRETS

Read It

"What do you think I gained by fighting wild animals in Ephesus? If the dead are not raised to life, 'Let's eat and drink. Tomorrow we die.' Don't fool yourselves. Bad friends will destroy you. Be sensible and stop sinning. You should be embarrassed that some people still don't know about God" (1 Corinthians 15:32-34).

Think It

How can "bad friends" end up destroying us? What's the smart thing to do when a friend acts more like a creeper than a friend?

Live It

Temptations and challenges are everywhere, even in places we least expect. That's why making the right friends and being the right kind of friend are important parts of growing a strong faith. Like it or not, "Bad friends will destroy you." Friends who cause you to stumble, make fun of you behind your back, leech onto you during the good times, and then split the scene when you need help aren't friends at all. Here's some good advice I'm learning: Extend a hand of friendship to someone only if you're able to be an unsinkable witness. But if you find yourself being pulled down or drowning in the company of lethal people, lose the friendship. Then "be sensible and stop sinning."

Jot a Thought or Dream Up a Minecrafty Masterpiece

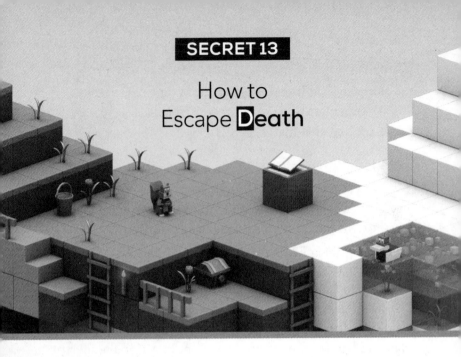

How to Escape **D**eath

I'm in survival mode, single player, exploring the rare Mesa (Bryce) biome.

This place is a harsh, alien world—what I imagine Mars to look like! Cacti and eerie dead bushes dot the landscape, and red sand stretches in every direction as far as the eye can see. But what I like the most are the hundreds of *hoodoos*—odd-shaped pillars of red rock that tower into the clear, blue sky. It's so strangely beautiful, I want to explore every inch of it.

Unfortunately, I can't.

I glance at the little gauge on my health bar and groan. "Oh no!" Only one heart is remaining, which means I'm starving! And earlier, I tumbled off a cliff and sustained some damage. And then I was attacked by spiders.

"Food—got to refuel and improve my health."

But it's too late for me. Just as I try to escape death...*POP!* My last heart disappears, and the words I dread flash on my screen: "Dragee90 starved to death."

Staying alive in survival mode isn't easy. If we're not careful, an exploding creeper or a bow-wielding skeleton can destroy our world and snuff out our lives. And as we explore amazing terrains, unexpected accidents can happen—such as tumbling off a cliff or falling into lava. Neglect is another killer. It's a silent one, but as you saw when I didn't pay attention to my health bar, it is every bit as dangerous.

In the real world, death is a scary subject, something I don't like to think about. Yet as a Christian, I have incredible news that I want to share with everyone: We can live forever! Through Jesus Christ we can escape eternal death and be with God in heaven...forever! How? Keep reading and pay close attention to today's Real-Life Secrets.

GAMEPLAY SECRETS

Death can occur both to a player and to mobs. It happens when the individual's health goes down to zero.

Dragee90's Best Tip

Each player receives two gauges that help them measure their success: a health bar with ten hearts and a food bar with ten drumstick-looking icons. Throughout gameplay these gauges rise and fall as you sustain damage or experience a victory. To avoid starving, I always keep food in my hotbar. Also, consider obtaining a splash potion to improve your health.

Read It

"Jesus then said, 'I am the one who raises the dead to life! Everyone who has faith in me will live, even if they die. And everyone who lives because of faith in me will never really die. Do you believe this?'" (John 11:25-26)

Think It

How does it make you feel to know that Jesus gives us eternal life with Him in heaven? How do we receive eternal life with Him?

Live It

Someday, whether by accident or illness or old age, each one of us will die. (Unless the Lord returns first!) Death stings. It's an enemy, not a friend—both of God and of man. Worst of all, death is the ultimate bad day for those who haven't accepted Christ as their Savior. If you're a Christian, you can be sure that your final heartbeat won't be the mysterious end to life. And when you stand at the graveside of a Christian brother or sister, you can receive comfort from knowing your loss is only temporary. That date when you and other believers meet Jesus face-to-face will be the ultimate homecoming. It will be the grand beginning to a life that never ends. How can we know for sure that we will spend eternity with God? Commit our lives to Jesus Christ. Pray this prayer right now:

Dear Jesus,

I agree that I am a sinner and that I need You. I believe that You are the Son of God and that You died on the cross to save me from sin and death.

Thank You for forgiving me. I want to repent and follow You. I want to commit my life to You right now.

Please come into my heart and be my Lord and Savior. Please fill me with Your Holy Spirit. Cleanse me, change me, and make me the person You want me to be.

I love You, Lord, and I thank You that I will spend all eternity with You.

In Jesus's name I pray. Amen.

Jot a Thought or Dream Up a Minecrafty Masterpiece

SECRET 14

Trading Diamonds for Clay?

I need a diamond chest plate, but I don't want to craft it myself or poke around a woodland mansion to find one. My best bet? Trade with a villager.

It's a misty morning in a plains biome, and I'm wandering through a medieval town that looks like a place right out of *The Hobbit*. A huge iron golem lumbers by—no doubt protecting villagers from hostile mob attacks.

The streets are buzzing with activity. Chickens cluck about freely, while pigs wallow in small pens. The townsfolk mill around in every direction, doing whatever it is that Minecraft people do. (I still haven't figured that out, but they seem busy!) I spot lots of characters in brown robes (farmers) and another guy wearing a purple outfit (a priest). The blocky, pixelated dude I'm searching for will be sporting a black apron, which sets him apart as a blacksmith.

"Bingo," I tell myself. "Just spotted my man."

I quickly check his menu and find what I need. "Yikes, your prices are high," I protest. "But I guess I have no choice. Got to make the trade."

I shell out 19 emeralds to acquire the chest plate. Suddenly, a purple particle effect appears over his head, which means he's offering a new trade. I check it out and smile. "Score! You're on, dude—let's keep trading."

The blacksmith offers to give me one emerald in exchange for three diamonds. To a Minecraft newcomer, that would sound like a crazy exchange—sort of like trading diamonds for clay. But to the seasoned player, it's a good deal. Emeralds are like currency in the game, and they are hard to obtain. And I just happen to have an abundance of diamonds.

We continue to trade this way until I have a healthy inventory of emeralds. I walk away feeling like a trading king!

I love finding treasure in Minecraft—whether it's a diamond, a chunk of gold, or an emerald. There's nothing more thrilling than swinging a pickaxe and discovering a long vein of precious gems. And I love stepping back and admiring the amazing things I've built, realizing that it all began with one simple block.

In life, God points us to the one thing we should treasure most: "'Love the Lord your God with all your heart and with all your soul and with all your strength and with all your mind'; and, 'Love your neighbor as yourself'" (Luke 10:27 NIV).

I leave the village, proud of my growing inventory and all the experience I'm gaining as a player. I now have the resources I need to expand Mount Quack and to advance to more challenging levels in the game.

Diamonds are valuable and very difficult to find, but if a player is fortunate enough to unearth them during gameplay, the crafting possibilities are endless.

Dragee90's Best Tip

A diamond is a strong and beautiful resource. I use it for armor, and I decorate my shelter with diamond blocks.

REAL-LIFE SECRETS

Read It

"Don't store up treasures on earth! Moths and rust can destroy them, and thieves can break in and steal them. Instead, store up your treasures in heaven, where moths and rust cannot destroy them, and thieves cannot break in and steal them. Your heart will always be where your treasure is" (Matthew 6:19-21).

Think It

What do you treasure most in life? What are some ways you can store up treasure in heaven?

Live It

The Bible says that the things that matter most to us are those we "store up" and spend time on: playing video games and sports, pursuing hobbies, earning money...the list is endless.

These things aren't bad; they're normal parts of everyday life. The question is, do our favorite activities and material things control us? Do we spend more time with our "treasures" than we do with our family...or getting to know God? But Scripture also says that if we use our time, talent, and money serving the Lord, then we're storing up treasure in heaven, which is a very good thing! God wants us to invest in things that help get people into heaven. It's the greatest investment of our lives.

Jot a Thought or Dream Up a Minecrafty Masterpiece

Avoiding a Dungeon Trap

I don't like dungeons, and I try to avoid them at all cost.

They're depressing places, nothing more than dark tombs with hard gray walls and floors made of mossy cobblestone. The rooms are tiny, and I always imagine the air to be sickening—like the musty smell of sadness.

Today, I'm standing at the entrance to one. I want to run, yet I'm curious...and I can't help taking a peek. *What makes these places so creepy?* I wonder as I linger a bit longer than I should. *Is this a trap? Is something luring me in?*

I hold up my torch and shudder. Chests line the walls, but they remind me of coffins. A mob spawner sits in the center of the room. And then it hits me: Dungeons are where monsters are born. Zombies, skeletons, and ugly, aggressive spiders enter Minecraft through these rooms.

Suddenly, I see something. It's a shadow...and then I hear a moan. Time to run!

My dungeon encounter reminds me of a night when I lingered on a scary TV show. As I flipped through channels, I stopped on a scene that involved a boy, a cemetery, and a coffin. *This looks bad,* I thought. *Better change the channel.* Yet I didn't. I was mesmerized. *What's going to happen next?* As the kid moved closer to the coffin...*CLICK.* My mom broke the spell. "Time to do homework," she reminded me. I was relieved.

Keep moving, I tell myself as I flee from the dungeon and continue my Minecraft mission: finding redstone ore so I can create circuits for my shelter. *Don't get stuck in fear...or pulled into a dungeon trap.*

GAMEPLAY SECRETS

Commonly found in caves, dungeons are easily spotted by the cobblestone and mossy cobblestone protective barriers that surround a mob spawner.

Dragee90's Best Tip

Stay alert as you explore these dark places because this is where zombies, skeletons, and spiders generate. Whenever I approach a dungeon, I pull out my diamond sword and keep it in my hand.

Read It

"You will give sight to the blind; you will set prisoners free from dark dungeons" (Isaiah 42:7).

Think It

What kinds of things in life scare you the most? How can Jesus set you free from fear?

Live It

We all have bad days. Sometimes we may feel stressed-out and scared...almost as if we're trapped in the creepiest of Minecraft dungeons. I've felt that way too, but thankfully my dad finds a way to pull me out of the fear. He begins by reminding me that Christians have a lot to celebrate. "Our faith is based on the unchangeable truth that God came to earth in Jesus, died for our sins, rose again from the dead, and even today reigns as Lord over all," Dad tells me. "Nothing can change this. Not feelings, not indigestion, not bad hair days, not lousy school days." My dad also points out that Jesus puts Himself in our shoes and feels everything we feel. That's pretty amazing! And when the Lord comes beside us and helps us out of our dungeons, He equips us to help others too.

Truth About the Enchantment Table

I've spent days building my amazing ice castle—Mount Frozen Quack.

I don't usually like the colder biomes, but this is pretty fun. I look out through my glass ceiling and see white mountains, big glaciers, and lakes of ice. Now it's time to check out my stockpiles in my chests. I've been gathering materials for days, and I can't wait to see what I can craft.

I grab three sticks and two pieces of string and craft a fishing rod. That will come in handy for ice fishing. I mix sugar, an egg, and a pumpkin to make a pumpkin pie. I combine iron ingots and redstone dust and create a compass. This will be useful when I'm trying to find my spawn point. And if I combine the compass with eight pieces of paper, I get a map. *Cool!* This is a great item to help me stay on course and avoid falling off a huge ice cliff. And I can't forget my armor. I want to upgrade from an iron set to a gold one. So I grab some gold blocks and go to work.

I know my recipes. And I know which elements to mix together to craft the items I need. But there's one item I don't like: the enchantment table. It's supposed to give my items more power and strength, yet there are no guarantees. When you place an item on the table, you're suddenly given several options that you can tap on. Here's the problem: Everything is written in a galactic alphabet. Even translating wouldn't help because the words are just decoration—they're random and pretty much meaningless.

It's a big gamble.

In the real world, beware of things that promise wealth and power. Especially when you must first give something up without knowing the potential outcome. Advertisers make all kinds of promises. Friends can sometimes pressure you into compromising situations. There are many traps for people who are looking for popularity and power. The Bible is full of these kinds of stories. Take your time. Do your research. Know where you're going before you take that first step. And always take time to pray. God will never lead you down the wrong path.

I stare at my enchantment table. *Hmm...what should I choose?*

Players must choose an option in the strange, meaningless language...and hope for the best. This really isn't for me. I like to know what I'm dealing with. It's just too risky to use my ingredients when I don't know where it's going to take me. So I pass.

GAMEPLAY SECRETS

These tables are strong—practically indestructible—and are sometimes found with tall, jam-packed bookshelves surrounding them. It's a place where the Lord of the Rings character Gandalf would feel at home. Magic happens here.

Dragee90's Best Tip

A tool or a weapon can be supercharged here, helping players gain an edge as they mine or face an enemy. But enchanting an item isn't easy, and it usually involves taking some risks.

REAL-LIFE SECRETS

Read It

"Many who were followers now started telling everyone about the evil things they had been doing. Some who had been practicing witchcraft even brought their books and burned them in public. These books were worth about fifty thousand silver coins. So the Lord's message spread and became even more powerful" (Acts 19:18-20).

Think It

What's most dangerous about evil practices like witchcraft? What can Christians do to steer clear of these activities—and to help others avoid them?

Live It

Sadly, the world is filled with misguided people who follow the occult. Their hearts have been darkened, and their minds have been tricked by deadly practices that God warns us to steer clear of. What kinds of things? Divination, sorcery, and witchcraft; channeling and seeking to talk with the dead; occult-related games like Ouija boards, crystal balls, tarot cards, and games such as Ka-Bala, ESP, or Telepathy. Even following horoscopes found in newspapers is off-limits because this is a form of astrology—another practice that leads people away from God.

In fact, occult practices can send people on a fast track straight to eternal darkness (hell). The evil spirits behind them use any kind of deception and dirty trick they can to gain control of a person's mind, body, and soul. So tell your friends not to fool around with this stuff. Once they invite a demon to lunch, there's a good chance it won't be leaving. Instead, "It is the LORD your God you must follow; and him you must revere. Keep his commands and obey him; serve him and hold fast to him" (Deuteronomy 13:4 NIV).

Jot a Thought or Dream Up a Minecrafty Masterpiece

Getting to the **End** (Which Is Really the Beginning)

I've built, fought, run, swum, jumped, crafted, grown, bred, and explored so much in Minecraft. And finally I've gathered, repaired, and constructed the correct elements to craft the End portal. I carried 12 Eyes of Ender straight into a stronghold. I constructed a ring of portal frame blocks around a 3x3 block. Then I placed an Eye of Ender in every end portal frame block. This activated the portal, and I gained access to the third and final stage of Minecraft—the End.

I look around this strange new world filled with a dim light that doesn't change. I'm standing on the center island, floating up and down as I gaze at several smaller islands in the distance. There have to be at least 1000 blocks between here and there. I grasp my compass, but it's not working. My clock isn't working either because there is no sun or moon. And I'm a little lost as I inspect the large obsidian platform that I'm standing on. There are several obsidian pillars surrounding the platform, each with an ender crystal on top. Some are just sitting there, and others are held into place with a cage or by bars.

Suddenly, I see the ender dragon flying in and out of the pillars. This is it. There's no turning back. I'm either going to slay this dragon or die trying.

Thankfully, I don't have to go into battle alone in real life. I am a child of God, and He is always preparing, training, and protecting me. Even when times are rough, I know He is my strength in all my battles—even the big one at the end. As long as I have the courage to take that step, God's power is what wins the battle.

Back in Minecraft, I've spent so much time and energy getting to the End. It's fun, and I've learned a lot. But it's crazy to think that it all comes down to this final battle.

It's risky, dangerous, and inevitable.

GAMEPLAY SECRETS

This is a special dimension of Minecraft that consists of an empty plane with a single floating island. But mostly, this eerie place holds the last challenge of the game: fighting the ender dragon. The only way out is to defeat it...or to die there.

Dragee90's Best Tip

The End is a creepy place where clocks and maps and compasses don't work. And don't even bother creating a bed there. If you do, it will explode! There's only one way out: Face the ender dragon.

Read It

"He will wipe all tears from their eyes, and there will be no more death, suffering, crying, or pain. These things of the past are gone forever. Then the one sitting on the throne said: I am making everything new. Write down what I have said. My words are true and can be trusted. Everything is finished! I am Alpha and Omega, the beginning and the end. I will freely give water from the life-giving fountain to everyone who is thirsty. All who win the victory will be given these blessings. I will be their God, and they will be my people" (Revelation 21:4-7).

Think It

What's your definition of *eternal life*? What does the Bible say? (For some clues, reread the verses above.) Share why you're excited to one day be in heaven with God.

Live It

I took a long, slow sip of cocoa and then gazed at the Colorado sky. "It's amazing here," I said to my dad. "A little piece of heaven."

Endless blue had given way to countless stars. Intense white lights skipped and danced around milky clusters of yellow and purple. Shooting stars raced across the horizon. For my dad and me, this is what camping is all about. Our time in the wilderness always has a way of deepening our faith...resetting our focus...reminding us that heaven will be even greater.

What will our eternal home be like? The Bible offers some snapshots. It will be...

a place of pure joy (Isaiah 25:8)

a safe haven (Ezekiel 28:24-26)

found through the narrow gate (Matthew 7:13-14)

an endless celebration (Luke 13:29-30)

a place where we live in peace with Jesus (Revelation 7:13-17)

Jot a Thought or Dream Up a Minecrafty Masterpiece

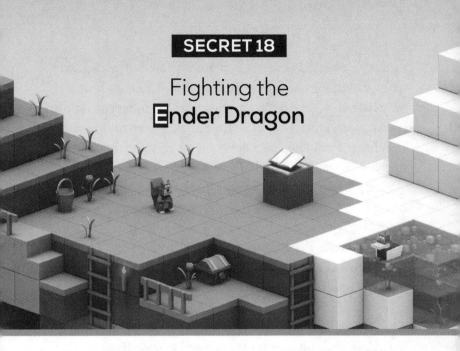

Fighting the Ender Dragon

I'm ready. I have my bow and sword, food, a pickaxe, some ender pearls, and some potions—Harming II, Swiftness II, Regeneration, and Healing II. I have two sets of armor, backup weapons, and a couple of pumpkins. That's right, pumpkins.

I jump off the obsidian platform and move toward the closest pillar. I grab my bow and take aim at the ender crystal sitting on top. I shoot and miss. I move a little to my right and try again. *Yes!* I nailed it.

But I see the ender dragon circling above, and it is not happy. It locks into my position and heads straight for me. I run to my right, but the edge is so close. I know not to get within ten blocks of the edge. If the dragon gets close enough it will use its knockback ability and shove me over. Not only will I die, but all of my supplies will be lost too. The last thing I want to do is fall into the void.

So I turn to my left and run for my life. I was so busy looking up that I almost didn't see the endermen all around me. I quickly look away, trying not to provoke them. It's going to be hard, so I switch strategies and replace my helmet with a pumpkin. I know it's not much protection, but it dramatically helps me avoid the endermen. I may look crazy, but now I can focus on the only way to defeat the dragon—by destroying all of the ender crystals.

I hop down a small ledge and head toward another pillar. But as I get close I realize that this crystal is protected by a cage. Great...what am I going to do now? I keep moving as I focus on another pillar in the distance. *WHACK!*

Suddenly, I'm flying through the air. *WHACK!*

I've been hit again—and it's all coming from the ender dragon. *How did he get here? Wasn't he way up in the sky?* But now it's as if he appears from nowhere. I run around as quickly as I can, trying to lose him. But he hits me again and again and again.

My health bar is almost out, and I'm so shaken that I can't remember what to do as the dragon gives his final blow. *POW!*

Sometimes the best experience is failure.

I know this isn't something we hear every day. Yet we gain knowledge from both success and failure. So we shouldn't be afraid to try new things. Most inventors have years of unsuccessful trials before their inventions work. Scientist can do thousands of experiments before proving a hypothesis. All of us get smarter every time we try something new—even if it doesn't work the first time. God gave us the gift of time. Time allows us to dream, explore, test, and discover our world.

It's great to be prepared, but we can't let fear keep us from getting out of our comfort zones and taking on a dragon or two!

This Minecraft battle is over. I thought I was prepared, but I just wasn't ready for the intensity of the ender dragon. That's okay. Tomorrow will be different.

GAMEPLAY SECRETS

The ender dragon is the game's ultimate bad creature. Players have to defeat it in order to escape a dimension called the End. (See the description in Secret 17.) And if they succeed, they are awarded a high honor: the End achievement—which means extra XPs (experience points) are added to their accounts...*and* they receive a permanent portal that grants them access to and from this dimension. But this honor comes at a high price.

Dragee90's Best Tip

Chaos erupts with endermen and purple stealthy shulkers joining the battle. The dragon will come at you, trying to strike you with its wings or spew ender acid on you. The situation may seem desperate, but I have a plan: Find all the towers in the End and knock them out. These places actually shoot beams that regenerate the ender dragon.

REAL-LIFE SECRETS

Read It

"Then the devil who fooled them will be thrown into the lake of fire and burning sulfur. He will be there with the beast and the false prophet, and they will be in pain day and night forever and ever" (Revelation 20:10).

Think It

What will happen to the dragon—that old snake who is also known as the devil? What do you think it will be like on that day when evil is crushed?

Live It

I'm not sure if Hollywood could dream up an epic scene this incredible. The ultimate battle between good and evil and the final defeat of Satan will be thrilling, chilling...and no doubt filled with thundering cheers from God's army. "I saw an angel come down from heaven, carrying the key to the deep pit and a big chain. He chained the dragon for a thousand years. It is that old snake, who is also known as the devil and Satan" (Revelation 20:1-2). And after a thousand years—*victory*! The devil will be crushed and defeated. Our Lord and His people—you and me—will win! Stay faithful. The tears and struggles we face today will turn into eternal smiles.

Jot a Thought or Dream Up a Minecrafty Masterpiece

SECRET 19

Avoid Eye Contact with an Enderman

What am I thinking? This is totally crazy!

I should stop right now. Yes—that's it. Just freeze and act invisible.

Pretend I was never here.

But it sees me. And now it's moving toward me. This is bad!

It's dusk, and I'm in a lonely field somewhere in a plains biome—tracking an enderman. Yep. Like I said...*crazy!* Usually players stay clear of these creepy mobs. But not me. Not today.

Endermen have the amazing ability to teleport, which makes them exceptionally dangerous. If they attack and you run...*POOF!* They teleport right in front of you. *POOF!* Now they're behind you. *POOF! THUMP!* Suddenly they're on you.

If that happens, it's game over.

But if you have the skills to defeat these rare creatures, you'll be nicely rewarded. The enderman will drop an ender pearl, and you'll rack up five XP orbs (which improve your gameplay level). And with the pearl, you too will have the ability to teleport.

That's why I'm acting like a crazed duck...determined to get the prize.

My thoughts run wild as the enderman moves toward me. I can't help thinking about my smart real-world friend who took a dumb risk. He tried to get his one minute of social media fame by juggling burning Nerf balls—live on Snapchat. Luckily, no one got hurt. But his reputation crashed and burned when his parents saw the video.

Back in the game, I decide to change plans. *It's just too risky to continue.* But just as I begin to retreat, the creature darts toward me. *Yikes!*

My face is covered with a pumpkin mask, which I've been told will prevent endermen from getting hostile. (Apparently endermen don't like to be stared at.) And so far it's working.

I've never been this close to one of these guys. It's a thin, dark creature with grotesquely long legs and arms and haunting eyes that glow in the dark. Strangely enough, it's holding a pumpkin block in its arms.

I'm ready to make my move with a bucket of water in one hand and my diamond sword in the other. My plan is to wound it with the water (liquids have that effect on these guys) and then strike it with my sword.

Yet before I can make a move, it begins to rain and...*POOF!* The enderman just teleports away. Would my plan have succeeded? I'll never know.

GAMEPLAY SECRETS

An Enderman is a tall, thin creature who becomes a bad guy if a player looks at or attacks it. These creatures are hard to destroy, and they make horrible noises. Yet they have stuff that everyone needs in order to get to the End and fight the ender dragon.

Dragee90's Best Tip

Endermen drop ender pearls, which players need. But watch out—they are hostile if you make eye contact with them, and since they can teleport, they're nearly impossible to escape. Here's a survival tip that can save your life: Don't ever try to destroy them with a bow and arrow. They manage to dodge arrows *every* time they encounter one. Instead, face them with a diamond sword.

REAL-LIFE SECRETS

Read It

"We are tempted by our own desires that drag us off and trap us. Our desires make us sin, and when sin is finished with us, it leaves us dead" (James 1:14-15).

Think It

How does temptation begin? Where can temptation lead us?

Live It

What can happen if we stare at temptation— lingering in its presence instead of turning away. It's sort of like making eye contact with an ender-man. It's as if an evil spell tricks us and consumes us. Our proximity to the temptation immobilizes our senses. It seems to own us. It often calls out to us—and when it presents itself, we are completely undone.

Scripture warns that temptation comes in many forms. Sometimes it's disguised as a friend. Sometimes it appears to be clothed in light—coming to us with seemingly innocent intentions. Temptation is always stealthy, always deceptive...kind of like a certain snake that entered a certain garden long, long ago. The solution: "Submit yourselves, then, to God. Resist the devil, and he will flee from you" (James 4:7 NIV).

Jot a Thought or Dream Up a Minecrafty Masterpiece

Experience
That Counts

Yes! I can't believe that I beat those crazy creepers. I stop at the top of the hill and take inventory. I used up some of my resources, but I gained a bunch of experience points, or XPs. Experience orbs are dropped when an attacker is killed, and they float in the air until collected. But this must be done within five seconds, or they will disappear.

Creepers follow me around and speed up the closer they get. The only things that can stop them are running water currents and spider webs. One by one, I collect the orbs, and the bar at the bottom of my screen gets a little bit fuller. Every time one is absorbed, a short bell rings. That's a good sound. Just a few more of these shiny little orbs and I'll achieve level 31.

Experience may not look like shiny little floating orbs in real life, but it is very valuable. Just as in the game, we gain experience through everyday activities. We learn as we go to school, do our chores, read our Bibles, hang out with friends, go to church, and play games.

Someone once told me, "I can tell you that glass breaks. But until you break a glass, you won't really know what that means."

We may not try to slay a dragon every day, but we can learn as we experience life. And we will continue to build that experience as we grow older. Just remember to use it to make better decisions and grow closer to Christ.

Back in the game, I've been doing everything I can to get my levels higher.

I've been breeding animals, fishing, killing slime, and using my furnace to craft various items. But defeating a hostile mob is definitely quicker. And defeating the ender dragon gives enough orbs to gain 12,000 XPs. That's more than 200 times more than any other creature in Minecraft. But that's not an everyday experience.

I could gain some through commands, but this action is limited. So I'll keep collecting experience points the old-fashioned way—by playing the game. And they sure will come in handy when I need to boost the power of my armor or repair my tools after a battle.

GAMEPLAY SECRETS

Players can rack up 17 XPs in each of the first 16 levels of the game. Points can be obtained by gathering experience orbs as they mine, as well as by doing all the usual Minecrafty activities: farming, fishing, gathering, smelting, building...defeating threats to their world. So what's the point of an experience point?

REAL-LIFE SECRETS

Read It

"When we were children, we thought and reasoned as children do. But when we grew up, we quit our childish ways. Now all we can see of God is like a cloudy picture in a mirror. Later we will see him face to face. We don't know everything, but then we will, just as God completely understands us. For now there are faith, hope, and love. But of these three, the greatest is love" (1 Corinthians 13:11-13).

Think It

What can help us to grow our faith? (For a clue, open your Bible and read Mark 12:30-31.) Describe someone in your life who is a strong Christian. What makes this person so strong?

Live It

Right now we're kids, but one day we want to grow into strong men and women of God. How do we get there? Step-by-step, choice by choice. My pastor says this: "Avoid the distractions that can hurt you,

and choose the paths that will help you grow and become a better, smarter person for God." Good advice. And just as experience makes a difference in Minecraft, it counts in life too. For Christians, here's the place to begin: Trust God. "'You must love him with all your heart, soul, mind, and strength.' The second most important commandment says: 'Love others as much as you love yourself.' No other commandment is more important than these" (Mark 12:30-31).

Jot a Thought or Dream Up a Minecrafty Masterpiece

Getting the Most out of Your **F**urnace

I swing my pickaxe with a fury as I gather cobblestone. I combine the blocks into a furnace and place it in a mine cart. Just like all furnaces, this one generates heat, smoke, and flames. But it's going to do so much more for me. I'm going to use it to smelt items into other, more useful, items. I can bake clay, char wood, smelt ores, and cook food with these furnaces.

I gather some wood, combine it with saplings (fuel), and place them in the furnace to craft charcoal. I know it's working because I see the light and the fire particles. I can close the menu and move on to my next task. But if the fuel runs out, it will stop smelting and I'll waste the burn time I have left. So I think I'll stick around until it's done—it only takes ten seconds. The arrow is at full, and the charcoal is put into my output field and an output item.

The last thing I want to do is go to bed. I learned the hard way that going to bed stops the clock and everything stops working.

And when I get up, the clock has been reset to morning. I totally wasted my fuel and ingredients the last time I tried this. So I'll stay awake this time.

Now that I have upgraded my tools, I can use my old, wooden tools as fuel. But coal or lava works so much better. I place a hopper on top of the furnace that will automatically feed the flames and empty the items. This is going to really help when I have larger jobs to do.

So I keep swinging my pickaxe and gathering more ingredients to be smelted. I need the charcoal to fuel my powered mine carts. But cooking food is the most important thing I'm going to do with my furnace. That's right—I've been breeding cattle, and they are going to make some amazing steaks. They also drop leather and more meat. And they are the best source of food to restore my hunger when it's getting low. Raw beef can restore my food bar by 1.5, whereas cooked beef restores it by 4. Pork chops are also a great source of food. Pigs are easy to breed and will produce a large amount of pork chops in short time. I may even occasionally make cookies or a cake. But those are just for fun since they don't restore the food bar very much. Back to work now—I need to stockpile more charcoal.

Building a furnace doesn't seem very exciting. But it's super cool when you think about all the items you can craft with one. Anytime fuel produces more fuel, that's going to help my future. And that's also the way I think about investing my time in real life. If I pour my time and energy into the right activities, I will benefit down the road. But if I spend all my time running around seeking only the exciting things, then I will not be prepared later.

For example, I can learn a lot from reading my Bible. Then, when I find myself in a difficult situation, I'm better prepared to react in a way that would make Jesus happy. But if I haven't invested my time in learning His ways, I will be totally lost in the face of confusion.

The simple things in life—and in Minecraft—are often so important.

GAMEPLAY SECRETS

Gourmet chefs use ovens the way experienced Minecraft players use furnaces. To be successful in the game, players have to turn blocks into other useful items. A furnace is the key.

Dragee90's Best Tip

Players add various combinations of blocks into furnaces and smelt them into amazing things. It's the key to building a cool world. I especially like to smelt sand blocks, turning them into glass blocks.

REAL-LIFE SECRETS

Read It

"Then I will purify them and put them to the test, just as gold and silver are purified and tested. They will pray in my name, and I will answer them. I will say, 'You are my people,' and they will reply, 'You, LORD, are our God!'" (Zechariah 13:9).

Think It

When we mess up, why is it important to go to God in prayer and tell Him we are sorry? How does God purify us?

Live It

Whenever my family and I visit Estes Park, Colorado, we always stop by this quirky little shop where glassblowers create fragile works of art. Globs of molten glass are heated in a furnace that reaches crazy hot temperatures—up to 2300 Fahrenheit! Using a long pipe, artists blow air into the glass and—*voila!*—colorful pieces are formed before our eyes: vases, goblets, bowls. At a jewelry shop in Denver, silversmiths custom design and create beautiful, one-of-a-kind bracelets, rings, and ornaments.

The artisans use a refiner's fire to purify the precious metal. The extreme high heat melts down a bar of silver, isolating the impurities that could ruin its value. It burns up those impurities and leaves the silver intact. I love watching these artists make something so incredible out of ordinary materials.

Know what? God is doing the same thing with our faith. He is like a refiner's fire—burning away the bad stuff from our lives (sin) and making us beautiful, holy, and pure.

SECRET 22

Thriving in Each Game Mode

I'm having a blast in creative mode as I jump from the ledge of my massive house and onto the top of my smaller cottage. I look around and see so many of my creations. There is a drawbridge in the distance and a vibrant farm to my left. But my favorite structure is my crazy roller coaster. Yep, I created a ride that is not for the faint of heart.

I began by crafting rails from iron ingots and sticks. For powered rails I used gold ingots, a stick, and redstone. I laid my wood planks down in a wild pattern to outline a ride with massive drops and breathtaking turns. It's my best build yet. One of the best things about creative mode is that there are endless building materials and no scary creatures to run from. It's a place where my imagination can run wild.

I sometimes jump over to adventure mode, but the only way to interact is with levers and buttons. I like the adventure maps, but I don't like that I can break blocks only with a destroy data tag. It's just not enough. And spectator mode is like flying around like an invisible creature. It's a great way to see what others are doing to survive, but it's not much on the interactive side.

But survival mode is a whole new world. It was a shock the first time I gave it a try. Suddenly, weird creatures were spawning from every corner. I was being chased around with no idea how to defend myself. I had to lose several battles before I learned the tricks of survival. It's fun in an entirely different kind of way. In this mode, crafting structures is about survival, not just creativity. Farming is about staying alive instead of just looking at colorful flowers and waterfalls. And elements are used for armor and weapons as well as crafting structures. There's even a game mode modifier called *hardcore* mode that permanently sets survival mode to *hard*. This is not for the faint of heart.

In the real world, I feel like I'm in creative mode when I'm at home or in church.

These are places where I can let my defenses down and just be myself. I can ask questions about God and faith without the threat of ridicule. I can slow down and let my creative juices flow. And I've learned that after spending some time in these safe zones, I'm better prepared for the adventure of survival.

In Minecraft, I like to take a break from survival mode and spend some time in creative. It's a great way to explore new crafting skills without worrying about hostile mobs.

GAMEPLAY SECRETS

Five game modes drive the fun in Minecraft: survival, creative, adventure, spectator, and hardcore.

Dragee90's Best Tip

Every mode is fun. In creative, you get to relax and spend all day building amazing things. But survival and hardcore are where you'll encounter nonstop action, and those two are my favorites. Here's a key to staying alert in survival mode: Turn up the volume on your computer—just slightly, but not too much—so you can hear more clearly what's about to attack.

REAL-LIFE SECRETS

Read It

"Always be joyful and never stop praying. Whatever happens, keep thanking God because of Jesus Christ. This is what God wants you to do" (1 Thessalonians 5:16-18).

Think It

Why does God want us to keep thanking him—even when life is hard? Why is it important to keep praying?

Live It

God wants us to be thankful in all circumstances—good times and bad. It's easy when life is good, but it feels almost impossible to stay happy when everything is messed up. A man in the Old Testament named Job knew this all too well. His life became miserable, and he ended up losing everything—his family, his health, his wealth. He became very stressed and pretty mad at God, yet he didn't turn away from the Lord. If you open your Bible to the very last chapter of Job—42:5 to be exact—you'll see what this broken man had to say: "I heard about you from others; now I have seen you with my own eyes."

Job stayed faithful—through good times and bad—and he gained a new appreciation of God's character, His holiness, and His sovereignty. Job learned to trust God even more, and his relationship with his Creator was deeper than ever. "Always be joyful and never stop praying." It's hard to do sometimes, but God will bless us if we try.

Jot a Thought or Dream Up a Minecrafty Masterpiece

SECRET 23

Deflecting a Ghast's Explosive Fireball

I strike my last glowstone block with my diamond pickaxe and smile. "Got what I came for," I tell myself, "now it's time to head home!"

And the sooner I get out of here, the better. I'm in the creepy, depressing dimension known as the Nether. It's the only place to find glowstone, a bright block that's anything but dreary. The warm, golden light from glowstone is a perfect way to brighten up a shelter.

Why does it have to grow here? I wonder. I look around the place and shudder. It's filled with fire, rivers of lava, and dangerous mobs like—

"Ghasts!" I scream.

Not again. Didn't I run into these guys the last time I was here?

A swarm of them are moving toward me. Their grey bodies are massive—the size of my real-world house—and they have long tentacles that dangle beneath them. They usually spend their days floating aimlessly around the Nether with their eyes and mouths shut.

But one of them just opened its eyes and is staring right at me. Suddenly, it makes some strange sounds, and then it begins to attack...

CHIRP! CHIRP! CHIRP! WHOOSH!

The ghast launches a fireball. I deflect it with my diamond sword and then race to my only way of escape—the portal.

The portal is what transported me here from the Overworld, and it's the way in and out of the Nether. Basically, a portal looks like a doorway with a black obsidian frame and a misty purple center. Airport gates in the real world are sort of like portals—without the mist, of course. You walk down a long ramp and through a door, and eventually you blast off to what feels like a different dimension—a new time zone and a different city.

Right now I have one destination in mind—Mount Quack!

I dive through the purple mist and land in my Minecraft shelter. But I have to act fast and destroy the portal. I don't want Nether monsters invading my world. So I slam my sword into the obsidian frame, and the portal breaks into pieces.

Whew! Think I'll find a better way to travel!

GAMEPLAY SECRETS

A ghast is a large, flying mob that players encounter in the Nether. The second these creatures lock eyes on someone, they blast away with explosive fireballs.

Dragee90's Best Tip

Keep your bow and arrow at the ready, because that's the best way to defeat a ghast. Its fireballs can be deflected by striking them, but it takes skill and expert timing to do so.

REAL-LIFE SECRETS

Read It

"You are tempted in the same way that everyone else is tempted. But God can be trusted not to let you be tempted too much, and he will show you how to escape from your temptations" (1 Corinthians 10:13).

Think It

How can we escape temptation? Do you believe that Jesus gives us the power to resist sin? (Please explain.)

Live It

Just as a ghast tries to hit us with an explosive fireball in the game, in real life Satan tries to trip us up with temptation and sin. So, when we find ourselves drawn to a sinful act—anything that would disappoint God—don't risk getting burned. Instead, take some advice from a firefighter:

Stop to consider the consequences.

Drop to your knees and pray.

Roll away from temptation.

SECRET 24

Don't Lose Your **G**lass Blocks

I feel like I've turned into a one-man glass-making machine. As fast as my hands and feet will move, I put sand in a furnace, heat it up with coal, and churn out glass blocks. Lots of them. Actually, dozens and dozens of them.

Remember the indoor swimming pool I'm adding to Mount Quack? (Flip back to Secret 11 for the full story.) The pool isn't quite finished, but the walls are up. Today I'm enclosing the massive complex with a huge glass ceiling. It's a *big* job. But when I'm finished, tons of light will flood the space, which—if you'll recall—includes a mini golf course, a tropical garden, and an NBA-worthy basketball court.

Now I have plenty of glass blocks in my inventory, so it's time to place them...which means becoming a robotic one-man block-placing machine.

First, I refer to my hotbar and select a block. Next, I place it by right-clicking my mouse. *CLICK*. And then I repeat the process...over and over and over. *CLICK*. *CLICK*. *CLICK*.

Pretty tedious, huh? But the end result is an amazing Minecraft creation that is well worth the hard work—an awesome vacation destination in my own Mount Quack!

My favorite real-world vacation was cruising through the Caribbean. Not too long ago, my family and I hopped aboard a huge ship and sailed through the Gulf of Mexico, eventually landing in the Bahamas. I practically lived on the pool deck—especially the outdoor basketball court. The sun and fresh sea air were amazing.

I love to swim, I love palm trees, and I *love* basketball. But even more, I love light. It makes me happy. It brings me to life and frees up my mind. That's why cruising is my ideal vacation, and it's why glass blocks are everywhere in my Minecraft house.

Yep—my indoor pool is now my favorite addition to Mount Quack.

Hmm...wonder where I can add more glass ceilings? Maybe a sky tower! Time to smelt more sand. Back to being a one-man glass-making machine.

GAMEPLAY SECRETS

Glass blocks are mostly used for aesthetics, but they also provide protection against mobs. Mobs can't break blocks—even the otherwise fragile glass ones. So how is this type of block made and used in the game?

Dragee90's Best Tip

Glass is created by smelting sand in a furnace. One block of sand yields one block of glass. But be careful—if you break it, you don't get the glass back. I use it to build windows, stained glass decorations in temples, swimming pools, and fountains. And here's a secret use for glass that can help you in survival mode: Monsters can't see through glass or ice blocks, so always include windows in your shelter. (I mentioned this in Secret 1.)

REAL-LIFE SECRETS

Read It

"No one lights a lamp and puts it under a bowl or under a bed. A lamp is always put on a lampstand, so that people who come into a house will see the light. There is nothing hidden that will not be found. There is no secret that will not be well known" (Luke 8:16-17).

Think It

Based on these verses, how is living for God like clicking on a lamp and putting it on a lampstand for all to see? Since nothing is hidden, how does God want us to live our lives?

Live It

God's goodness illuminates the darkness. In fact, He wants His light to shine so brightly through us, others will want to follow Him too.

And as His children, the Lord wants us to be transparent—with Him and with each other. Everything we say, everything we do, everywhere we go, every thought we think...the Lord knows them all. Nothing can be hidden from Him.

> There is nothing concealed that will not be disclosed, or hidden that will not be made known. What you have said in the dark will be heard in the daylight, and what you have whispered in the ear in the inner rooms will be proclaimed from the roofs (Luke 12:2-3 NIV).

Jot a Thought or Dream Up a Minecrafty Masterpiece

Maximizing Glowstone

If you need a super bright light that's anything but boring, glowstone is your ticket. It just looks so interesting. The block is speckled with little patches of yellow, tan, brown, and green. I can't stop looking at it! The middle of my ceiling in Mount Quack's grand room is covered with glowstone, making it the brightest, grandest grand room in my world.

But I have to warn you—getting your hands on this block is the hard part. Either you trade with a village cleric, or you hunt for it in the Nether.

Ugh...the Nether.

Glowstone is in abundance there, so it's the quickest way to build up your inventory. Yet I can't stand going anywhere near that gloomy, dangerous place. It's filled with fire and lava...and hostile mobs that constantly attack. Unlike a mineshaft, there's something so empty and chilling about the Nether. It reminds me of a real place that's mentioned in the Bible—a place that's even creepier but that Jesus helps us avoid. (Can you think of what I'm talking about?)

As I suit up and prepare for my journey there, a puzzling question nags at me: *Isn't it strange that such a happy light gets its start in such an unhappy place?*

Recently, my family and I got to serve at an inner-city church in Saint Louis. The neighborhood was really poor—broken-down houses, broken-down cars, and broken-down people. But right in the middle of the sadness was a bright light—a church that served God, and Christians who brought smiles and joy and eternal hope to the community. *It's a little like finding glowstone in the Nether,* I thought.

Back in the game...

I find the blocks I've been searching for. Coral-like clusters of glowstone hang from the undersides of netherrack—a dark, purple-speckled block that (if lit on its topside) can burn forever. I move in and gather some glowstone blocks. *Better hurry before a mob attacks.*

GAMEPLAY SECRETS

This type of block is found naturally only in the Nether, and it's very useful since it generates light. When it is broken with a pickaxe, it produces light-stone dust, not to mention a light level of 15.

Dragee90's Best Tip

Level 15 is the game's brightest degree of light. It's a great way to illuminate a cave or your shelter. And here's how I maximize the use of glowstone: I decorate my house with it. I prefer it to torches.

REAL-LIFE SECRETS

Read It

"Once again Jesus spoke to the people. This time he said, 'I am the light for the world! Follow me, and you won't be walking in the dark. You will have the light that gives life'" (John 8:12).

Think It

How is Jesus the "light for the world"? (Please explain.) How can we keep from walking in the darkness?

Live It

You and I can be like glowstone in the dark places of this world—at school, in our communities...everywhere. Now more than ever our friends need encouragers—Christians who show kindness, godly kids who are willing to love those who have been wounded by discouragers. Ask the Lord to show you what to do and whom to help. In the Bible, Jesus reaches out to the unlovable, befriends those the world would rather forget, and helps those who seem helpless.

What to Stock in Your Inventory

I open my inventory screen and do a little Minecraft victory dab.

"Yep—I've definitely been a busy duck," I say with a smile. "And Mount Quack's pool will soon be filled with water blocks and a certain feathered warrior splashing around."

My indoor garden-pool-mini-golf-basketball complex will soon be a reality! Well, technically it'll be a virtual-reality reality. But I'm pretty sure I have all the resources I need to finish the job. Just to be sure, I count my supply...

- Food? Check. *Wheat—30. Apples—10. Potatoes—35. Carrots—20. Melons—64.* (Yeah, I know. I'm kind of crazy about watermelon!)

- Foliage? Check. *Grass—50. Leaves—64. Flowers— 30. Fern—47.*

- Wood? Check. *Spruce—37. Jungle—50. Dark Oak—20.*

- Stone? Check. *Cobblestone—52. Basic stone—60. Sand—64.*

- Ore? Check. *Coal—57. Iron—33. Redstone—42.*

- My "precious"? Check. *Gold—24. Diamond—28. Emerald—16.*

No doubt about it, my inventory is very good, both to survive in the game and to create cool things. And it didn't happen overnight. Adding stuff to your inventory involves mining, farming, gathering, hunting, exploring, crafting.

I've learned that as we collect the blocks we need to build an amazing world, no player should be skimpy with their inventory. Remember, each of the 27 storage slots holds up to 64 items. That's a lot. Now it's time to get busy and start building—block by block!

My real-world inventory changes with each activity and assignment. For school, it might be filled with textbooks, calculators, and notepads. For lacrosse, it centers on a stick, a ball, a helmet, and pads. A well-stocked inventory means having the right resources to get the job done.

Back at Mount Quack, I go to work on my indoor garden-pool paradise, placing my foliage blocks: grass, leaves, flowers, ferns. I have everything I need to make something cool!

Just as in real life, Minecraft players must keep an inventory of items at their fingertips—resources, food, tools, weapons.

Dragee90's Best Tip

Our inventory is what we use in creative mode to build our Minecraft worlds. It's also where we turn in survival mode for weapons and tools we need to defend ourselves. Always keep these basic items in your inventory: (1) a sword, (2) food, and (3) basic blocks to build with.

REAL-LIFE SECRETS

Read It

"The Spirit has given each of us a special way of serving others. Some of us can speak with wisdom, while others can speak with knowledge, but these gifts come from the same Spirit. To others the Spirit has given great faith or the power to heal the sick or the power to work mighty miracles. Some of us are prophets, and some of us recognize when God's Spirit is present. Others can speak different kinds of languages, and still others can tell what these languages mean. But it is the Spirit who does all this and decides which gifts to give to each of us" (1 Corinthians 12:7-11).

Think It

How has God gifted you? (Please explain.) How does He want us to use the many gifts He has given us?

Live It

Close your eyes and imagine all the things you can create and do in life. Don't hold back— just dream. What things make you happy? Which dreams has God put in your heart? Are you an artist or a scientist? A singer or a soldier? Pray about the gifts God has given you. Ask the Lord to reveal what His "good, pleasing, and perfect will" for your life looks like (Romans 12:2 NIV).

Talk with your parents and ask them to be your mentors. Let them know about your dreams. Their input will be valuable in helping you to follow your heart...and to grow into the exact person God wants you to be.

Jot a Thought or Dream Up
a Minecrafty Masterpiece

The Ultimate Way to Use a **L**adder

A ladder never looked so good in my life!

I hop on to it and climb like crazy—my legs nothing more than a spinning blur, my arms flailing, pushing, and pulling. I move so fast, I barely take a breath. And before I know it...light. I'm finally back on the surface, safe in my shelter. My mineshaft nightmare is well behind me.

So, what happened? And how did a simple ladder make the difference between life and death?

Seconds earlier, I was being chased by a spider jockey— and I barely dodged its barrage of flying arrows. Of all the monsters I've faced in Minecraft, this one will be hard to forget. It all happened so suddenly...

I was deep in my mine, tapping into a beautiful vein of gold ore. At first, all I saw was a couple of glowing red eyes in the shadows.

"Uh-oh. I have visitors."

But something told me this wasn't just any hostile mob. The red dots suddenly became red streaks. "It's moving toward me. Time to run!"

WHOOSH!

An arrow flew past me. And then a second and a third. I glanced over my shoulder and saw it—a spider jockey. It's basically a bow-wielding skeleton that rides on the back of a giant, creepy spider. It spawned this way and can jump, climb walls, and shoot arrows with precision. My best response? Put distance between me and this dangerous duo.

I tore through the tunnel and made a mad dash for my life. That's when I spotted the sweetest, most perfect mode of escape.

"Ladders rule!"

Every time I climb a ladder in the game, my mind goes back to the ones I've scaled in real life. At Colorado's Mesa Verde National Park, wooden ladders let you descend into ancient cliffside houses and underground rooms. As you crawl through dusty, tight spaces, you can't help being blown away by the amazing Minecraft-worthy craftsmanship. And then it hits you: This place was built by Pueblo ancestors 700 years ago...yet most of the houses are still standing strong!

One of the most popular villages in the park—a site called Cliff Palace—resembles a primitive castle made out of mud, stone, and wood. And everything was constructed on the side of a steep canyon wall. Look off the side and...*gulp*...your stomach will do flip-flops. For modern-day visitors, crude wooden ladders really do mean the difference between life and death!

Back at Mount Quack, ladders definitely rule. Some lead to towers that rise high above the landscape; others take you into deep underground rooms and mineshafts. And each one provides a quick escape from the game's creepy-crawlies.

GAMEPLAY SECRETS

Place seven sticks in a crafting grid and...*voila!* You just made a ladder. Ladders are primarily used to scale walls, but they have a couple of other uses.

Dragee90's Best Tip

Ladders will stop a stream of water when placed on an adjoining block. Also, they are useful in underwater construction. And when you place one on a block underwater, the ladder will create a block of breathable air.

REAL-LIFE SECRETS

Read It

"In a dream he saw a ladder that reached from earth to heaven, and God's angels were going up and down on it" (Genesis 28:12).

Think It

What do you think the ladder in Genesis 28 represents? Why were angels going up and down on it? What do you suppose they were doing? Do you think God actually speaks to people in dreams? (Please explain.)

Live It

In Genesis 28:10-19, a man named Jacob had a dream about an incredibly tall ladder that stretched all the way to heaven. And God spoke to Jacob in that dream:

> I am the LORD God who was worshiped by Abraham and Isaac. I will give to you and your family the land on which you are now sleeping. Your descendants will spread over the earth in all directions and will become as numerous as the specks of dust. Your family will be a blessing to all people. Wherever you go, I will watch over you, then later I will bring you back to this land. I won't leave you—I will do all I have promised (Genesis 28:13-15).

The ladder represented Jacob's connection with God. Guess what? We have that same connection too. "Jesus answered, 'I am the way and the truth and the life. No one comes to the Father except through me'" (John 14:6 NIV). Jesus is our Savior, who went to the cross and paid the price for our sins. When we commit our hearts to Him, we become friends with God...and we get to spend eternity with Him. So in a sense, the cross is like the ultimate ladder!

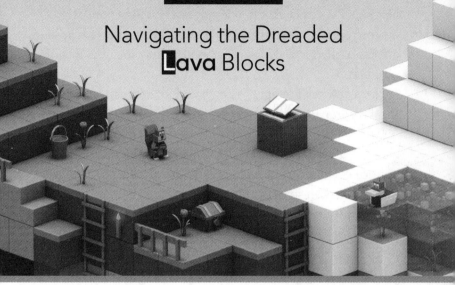

SECRET 28

Navigating the Dreaded Lava Blocks

I make my way through a dimly lit mineshaft, climb down a steep ladder, and step into a large, open cavern. Just ahead, a warm yellow-orange fog rises from the floor. And next to the glowing pit is a fast-moving waterfall. I hear popping, sizzling sounds as the current tumbles over a jagged stone wall and into the abyss.

I sniff the air and imagine a mixture of smoke and sulfur.

"Yep—this is where water and lava meet," I tell myself, "which means I'm about to score a healthy supply of obsidian blocks. Nice!"

Obsidian is perfect for building explosion-resistant structures, like bunkers. And I just happen to be building one at Mount Quack. I pull out my diamond pickaxe (the only tool that can mine this stuff) and move in for a closer look.

But suddenly the solid ground gives way to a narrow rock bridge—sort of like the fragile structures I've seen at Arches

National Park in Utah. On one side is a bubbling pool of lava, and on the other is a churning waterfall. Where the two meet are the dark, purple blocks I'd hoped to find: lots and lots of obsidian.

"Love it when I'm right," I laughed. "But how can I navigate the lava, grab the goods...and live to tell the tale?" And then it hits me: "Time for some ninja duck parkour action!"

I get a running start, springboard off the rock bridge, bounce off the cavern wall, grab some blocks as I fly over them...and then somersault onto a ledge.

"I'm still alive," I scream.

Now for my next challenge—getting off the ledge!

The best place to see lava in the real world is Kilauea Volcano on the island of Hawaii. To this day, it constantly erupts at its summit and at a spot called the Pu'u 'Ō'ō vent on its east rift zone. But if you ever visit this place, be careful. Venturing to the areas where the lava oozes into the ocean is hazardous. The lava touching the water triggers an explosion, which spews deadly flying debris. You're much better off viewing the action on webcam images.

But in Minecraft, being near lava is just a normal part of living in our blocky virtual world...so navigating it is important. That's why I keep a bucket of water handy. It can be a lifesaver, along with a few other important tricks.

GAMEPLAY SECRETS

Lava is a fluid block that can be used as a light source, a barrier, or as a weapon.

Dragee90's Best Tip

Be careful when working with lava blocks. Even if you're wearing armor, every second counts if you come in contact with it. There are plenty of places where you can find lava, and nearly endless ways to use it. Here's one of my favorites: I lure a monster troop toward me, and then I place lava between us. They almost always walk right into it.

REAL-LIFE SECRETS

Read It

"When you see trouble coming, don't be stupid and walk right into it—be smart and hide. Respect and serve the LORD. Your reward will be wealth, a long life, and honor. Crooks walk down a road full of thorny traps. Stay away from there!" (Proverbs 22:3-5).

Think It

What kinds of trouble does God want us to avoid? (Please explain.) How can we be smart if we're in a dangerous situation? How does God reward us?

Live It

Too many kids focus on the thrill of the moment, not the big picture. It's crazy when you think about it, but sometimes we're willing to risk getting in trouble—or hurting others—just to impress our friends. And we mistakenly believe that measuring up or being cool means following a cruel code: "Make fun of anyone who seems weak or different...and always do what the crowd says is right." But the Bible says something very different:

> God loves you and has chosen you as his own special people. So be gentle, kind, humble, meek, and patient. Put up with each other, and forgive anyone who does you wrong, just as Christ has forgiven you. Love is more important than anything else. It is what ties everything completely together (Colossians 3:12-14).

Jot a Thought or Dream Up a Minecrafty Masterpiece

SECRET 29

Mooshrooms and Other Oddities

Ever been to a mushroom island biome?

It's as if Willy Wonka and the cast of *Yo Gabba Gabba!* logged onto the same server and dreamed up their ideal vacation spot. A hilly, gray-brown landscape is filled with giant mushrooms (instead of grass and trees). And the ground is made up of sporelike blocks called *mycelium*. But the strangest part of the island is its native creature—*mooshrooms*! These are lumbering red-and-white-spotted cows with mushrooms growing on their backs and heads.

I walk up to a pair and offer them some wheat. Suddenly, they begin to multiply. And when a baby mooshroom chomps on some, it begins to grow bigger right before my eyes. But the weirdness doesn't stop there. When I right-click on a mooshroom while holding an empty bowl, I end up with lunch—a big serving of mushroom stew!

Can you imagine a stranger place? Actually, that's the

best part of Minecraft—encountering oddities like mooshrooms...and then dreaming up our own creations.

I get pretty bored with anything that seems too serious and too normal. I like being creative! My dad is an author and my mom is a children's pastor, so creativity naturally surges through my veins. When I'm not playing Minecraft or shooting hoops with friends, I draw, write, sing, dance, explore, collect, dream...imagine! It makes life in the real world so much fun.

GAMEPLAY SECRETS

Mooshrooms are rare Minecraft cows that spawn only in mushroom biomes. They're red-and-white, with red mushrooms growing on their backs. Like normal cows, mooshrooms drop zero to two pieces of leather, one to three pieces of raw beef (or cooked beef if it dies by fire), and experience orbs worth one to three XPs.

 Dragee90's Best Tip

Mooshrooms can jump up only one block and will try to do so when a block is in their way. Their AI isn't very advanced, as they'll walk into fires, but they will avoid high falls. When you attack a mooshroom, it will run, making it tricky to hit him again. It often runs in circles, however, so you won't have to walk too far to hit it again.

REAL-LIFE SECRETS

Read It

"Moses said to the people of Israel: 'The LORD has chosen Bezalel of the Judah tribe. Not only has the LORD filled him with his Spirit, but he has given him wisdom and made him a skilled craftsman who can create objects of art with gold, silver, bronze, stone, and wood. The LORD is urging him and Oholiab from the tribe of Dan to teach others. And he has given them all kinds of artistic skills, including the ability to design and embroider with blue, purple, and red wool and to weave fine linen'" (Exodus 35:30-35).

Think It

God gives us the ability to use our imaginations. In what ways is the Lord creative? How has He made you creative? (Share some of your creative abilities.)

Live It

All creativity flows from God. He is the original source of all we know. And we were created in His image. Therefore, He totally expects us to use our own creativity in our lives. So don't hold back. Find ways to explore new ideas as you explore your world. Just imagine how we can impact our culture with new and exciting ways to show others God's love. The Lord loves His children and guides our steps: "I will bless you with a future filled with hope—a future of success, not of suffering" (Jeremiah 29:11).

Beware of a
Monster Spawner

I'm exploring an abandoned mineshaft in a mesa biome, moving extra slowly down a long corridor. I can't take any chances today because this is "cave spider central"—a place filled with dozens of these hostile, dark-blue creatures. They pop out of nowhere, leaping on players and stinging them with poison.

It's a creepy place. Above me are oak supports holding up the ceiling. The walls are lined with torches, and the floor is covered with broken rails. But just ahead, I spot what I've been searching for—mine carts with chests...and plenty of loot inside.

"Eureka!" I shout. "This little adventure is going to pay off nicely."

That is, if I survive it.

I discover four chests filled with things I need: torches, bread, coal, melon seeds, pumpkin seeds, iron ingots, gold ingots, golden apple, diamonds, redstone...and much more. But I see something else that makes me groan—cobwebs.

And where there's a cobweb, there's bound to be a—

"Spider!" I yell. I swing my diamond sword just in time and strike it as it leaps through the air. "That was close." One down, but many more will come, so I'd better hurry.

Behind the thick mound of cobwebs is a striped, cagelike block called a *monster spawner*. And something is inside it—ready to generate.

"A cute little piglet maybe?"

Nope. It's another fanged fiend. I grab the loot and run!

I've often thought there's a mini monster spawner in each of us. It's that selfish "ping" that tries to pull us in the wrong direction. "Go on," it whispers, "nobody will know. Just do it!" It churns and spins in our thoughts, urging us to let the monster out. And if we do...*ouch*! We usually get stung.

But our inner monster spawner can be stopped. Not in our own power, of course, but through Jesus. All we have to do is call out to Him: "Jesus, I need help! Take away the temptation. Give me the strength to avoid sin...and to please You."

GAMEPLAY SECRETS

Monster spawners are found in dungeons surrounded by cobblestone and mossy cobblestone. They continually spawn a specific mob type, which appears as a spinning miniature version inside the monster spawner itself until sufficient light is placed around the spawn area. They can be broken, but once they are broken they are gone forever.

Dragee90's Best Tip

Monster spawners become active when a player is within a radius of sixteen blocks from the spawner. You need them for success in the game. Here's how I use monster spawners: I knock out the hostile creatures that spawn in them and rack up XPs.

REAL-LIFE SECRETS

Read It

"We know that the persons we used to be were nailed to the cross with Jesus. This was done, so that our sinful bodies would no longer be the slaves of sin. We know that sin doesn't have power over dead people. As surely as we died with Christ, we believe we will also live with him" (Romans 6:6-8).

Think It

What did Jesus do so that we are no longer slaves to sin? How have we "died with Christ"? How can we live with Him?

Live It

The power of sin is broken in our lives when we commit our hearts to Jesus. So whenever we mess up, we should never ignore the sin or think we can hide it from God. Instead, we must come clean with Him. Tell Him all about the stuff you've done wrong, and tell Him you're sorry. He'll forgive you. "If we confess our sins, he is faithful and just and will forgive us our sins and purify us from all unrighteousness" (1 John 1:9 NIV). Once you've confessed the sin and asked Jesus to help you change (that's called *repentance*), you can stop flogging yourself. You're totally forgiven—and free! Now with your relationship fully restored with God, you can take steps toward growth and change. The Holy Spirit will help you.

Jot a Thought or Dream Up a Minecrafty Masterpiece

SECRET 31

Know What's Hidden Near Mossy Cobblestone

I raise my torch and light up the entrance to a jungle temple. Incredible!

Strange and mysterious rooms come into view, and my imagination runs wild. I envision ancient Minecraft people who once lived here—warriors, kings...explorers like me.

But the best part? No cobwebs, no spiders...and not a single mob spawner. The place looks monster-free! So I concoct a simple plan: Swoop in, find the chest, raid the goodies, fend off any unexpected creepy-crawlies that may have followed me, and race out faster than you can say, "Indiana Jones!"

I take my first step and then my second. I move my torch in a long, slow arc, studying every nook and cranny—looking for the tiniest sign of danger. But all I see is mossy cobblestone. It's everywhere: the walls, the floor, the ceiling. And straight ahead are two sets of stairs. *Should I head up...or down?*

Down.

The lower chamber looks the same: more cobblestone, more mysterious possibilities. But this room is bigger, with twisty green vines that dangle from the ceiling. My eyes instantly zero in on a lone object sitting in the corner. It's a chest.

"Payday comes early," I say with a grin. And then my smile fades. "Wait...this is just *too* easy..."

I tilt my torch left and then right. "Sometimes a monster egg is hidden near mossy cobblestone," I warn myself. "And where there's a monster egg, there are bound to be silverfish. Dozens of them. Yikes!"

Just thinking about these annoying buglike creatures makes me shiver. They move fast *and* they're deadly. If one decides to attack and a player fights back, it calls its buddies and tries to overwhelm its prey.

So what should I do?

I continue to weigh my options. "But it's just so beautiful here," I reason. "Maybe I'll be okay. Besides, most silverfish hang out in the extreme hill biomes, and I'm in the jungle."

I begin to take a step but freeze in my tracks. That little pang inside tells me something isn't quite right. Suddenly, it hits me: The temple is a trap.

I spot hinged doors on the ground and tripwire lines. And I'm positive something is hiding in the shadows—perhaps just behind the vines or wedged between the mossy cobblestone.

Hmm...beautiful on the outside yet deadly on the inside. Danger lurking in the shadows, hidden from sight. A trap!

This describes a lot of things in the real world, doesn't it? Places, ideas, even people. I know I've talked about this a lot, but it's an important lesson I'm beginning to understand...and really want to share with you: *Go beyond the surface and look for hidden traps.* What seems right at first—an invitation from a friend, an idea, a place to visit—may be a really bad choice. So weigh the facts and uncover the truth. Ask for your parents' help with this. I do!

I slam my pickaxe on the ground as I race into the room. *CRUNCH! CLANG!*

The trapdoors fling open, but I leap into the air and hop right over the open pits. Just then, a volley of arrows launch from the vines.

WHOOSH!

I barely escape their sharp blades, only to face yet another challenge. As if on cue, a silverfish scampers toward me. I must have cracked open a monster egg when I slammed my pickaxe into the ground.

Somehow, I grab the loot and escape unharmed.

Yep—Indy would be proud!

GAMEPLAY SECRETS

This block looks exactly like cobblestone but with a green moss growing on it. It's mostly found in jungle temples and dungeons surrounding mob spawners. On a rare occasion, it may naturally show up in the Mega Taiga biome. This may look like any other cobblestone wall, but—just as I discovered—hidden dangers often lurk in and near these blocks.

Dragee90's Best Tip

The mossy cobblestones look soft and comfortable—and they're beautiful to look at. But don't be lured in by their looks. Beware of monster eggs and silverfish.

Read It

"Watch out for false prophets! They dress up like sheep, but inside they are wolves who have come to attack you. You can tell what they are by what they do. No one picks grapes or figs from thornbushes. A good tree produces good fruit, and a bad tree produces bad fruit. A good tree cannot produce bad fruit, and a bad tree cannot produce good fruit. Every tree that produces bad fruit will be chopped down and burned. You can tell who the false prophets are by their deeds" (Matthew 7:15-20).

Think It

Have you or your family ever met someone who posed as a good person on the outside but who actually wanted to trick people? (Please explain.) How does the Bible describe these kinds of people? What will happen to them? (Hint: Look at the second-to-last sentence in the Scripture passage above.)

Live It

What do these things have in common?

the Internet and being online

mossy cobblestone and jungle temples

today's Bible passage about false prophets

The answer can be summed up in one word: *deception*. There's a lot of that buzzing around our WiFi hotspots. The Internet is definitely a mind-boggling megalopolis of cyber-circuitry—something our grandparents would never have thought possible when they were kids. But along with the good stuff, it contains a gushing cybersewer that can invade our minds and trap us if we're not careful. And there are plenty of wolves dressed up like sheep who want to attack us. How can you stay safe?

Use God's Word to help you sort out right from wrong. Read Psalm 101:3; 2 Corinthians 10:5; and Philippians 4:8. Print them out and place them on your monitor as a constant reminder.

Use a computer that's positioned in an open place. Suggest to your parents that they create a computer workspace in a common area, such as the kitchen or family room.

Talk to Mom and Dad. If something doesn't seem right, tell them immediately.

Jot a Thought or Dream Up a Minecrafty Masterpiece

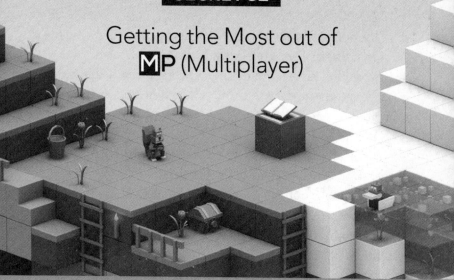

Getting the Most out of MP (Multiplayer)

With only moonlight to guide me, I'm running through an extreme hills biome.

My real-world friends Zach, Abby, and Eddy (AKA Daffy, Techgirl, and Awesomecupcake) are just a few steps behind me. We're on Zach's server in multiplayer, fighting to survive the night.

Somehow we've awakened the monsters, and they're in full force—bent on having us for dinner. A growing, growling army of them chase us down steep cliffs and through forests of spruce. Skeletons fling their arrows, spiders leap from the shadows, and zombies try desperately to bump into us.

"Quick!" Daffy yells through his headset. "My bunker. The door is right next to the torch."

CLICK, CLICK, CLICK.

I wildly tap my mouse and head for the light. Daffy flings open the door, and one by one we dive into safety.

CLICK.

The door slams shut, and we let out sighs of relief.

"That was insane," I tell Daffy. "But we're safe now."

"I couldn't fight them off any longer," Techgirl chimes in. "But Awesomecupcake took out a bunch of spiders with his sword."

"Way to go, Cupcake," Daffy shouts.

I look around the bunker and then alert my friends. "Uh, guys...where is Cupcake? He's not with us."

Daffy looks out the window and laughs. "That's because he's dancing with zombies."

Awesomecupcake is a madman who loves to pull crazy stunts like that. Right now he's outside, zigzagging through the trees—hopping, leaping...mocking the monsters and then running like crazy.

"He's nuts, but he's our friend, and we can't leave him alone in the woods," I insist. "It's go time."

My friends and I have each other's back in the game...and in real life. We share a bond and totally trust each other. We see each other at church and at school, and we're kind of like family to each other.

And that's one of the best parts of Minecraft: We get to enjoy it with family and friends. It's totally social—and I love that. It gives us a place where we can dream and create and live out crazy adventures with each other.

But the social part can be dangerous too—and not because of the make-believe monsters we face. I'm talking about the real ones who can log on to a server. So there are a few things I do to stay safe and to have fun in the game. Like what? Keep reading...

As you can see, multiplayer allows us to join friends and other Minecraft players from around the world. The server saves the world we create so we can continue the game the next day. The Internet is filled with lots of servers that offer a wide range of experiences. Some feature different versions of the standard Minecraft game—from older ones to the latest—and some let you play different kinds of games: Skywars, Skyblocks, Minecraft Hunger Games, capture the flag...you name it.

Dragee90's Best Tip

Ask your parents to help you find the right server to join. Be a detective and investigate them before you log on. Better yet, join a private server that a friend has set up, and play with only kids you know. Above all, *never* tell strangers your real name or where you live.

REAL-LIFE SECRETS

Read It

"They spent their time learning from the apostles, and they were like family to each other. They also broke bread and prayed together. Everyone was amazed by the many miracles and wonders that the apostles worked. All the Lord's followers often met together, and they shared everything they had" (Acts 2:42-44).

Think It

In what ways are your friends at church like family? Do you think it's important for Christ-followers to meet together regularly? Why or why not?

Live It

I love hanging out with my friends, especially the ones I see at church. The Bible tells us that "breaking bread" with our friends and church family is important. Here's why:

Attending church gives us a chance to worship with all kinds of people—young and old, rich and poor, people who go to your school and people who don't.

When we're at church, we can be fed from God's Word.

Going to church allows us to serve others.

It's a good habit to develop early in life. Someday, church may be the only way to experience good Christian fellowship, enjoy worship, and study the Word (see Hebrews 10:24-25).

SECRET 33

Don't End Up in the Treacherous Nether

Today, I think I'll kick things up a notch and jump over to the Nether.

I've been there before, and I don't like it very much. But it's where I find Nether quartz blocks to build walls and furniture, not to mention netherrack for my fireplaces and glowstone for lights at Mount Quack. (Other great stuff includes soul sand, blaze rods, and even some ghast tears.)

Whenever I visit, I spawn into a scary world of red rock, fires, and spooky sounds. All I want to do is grab my stuff and get out. And with each visit, I know I'm in danger. There are strange mobs here, and I'm not sure how to defeat some of them.

Suddenly, fireballs fly past my head. It's not hard to find the blaze—a bright pillar of smoke—against this dark world's landscape. There are 12 rods rotating around it as the pillar moves away. But it's still throwing balls of fire my direction.

I go into survival mode and try to deflect one fireball that's coming straight for my head, but it doesn't work. *Ouch!* It nails me.

I turn and run for my life. But I step into a hole and fall into a lava pit. This is not my day. As I respawn, I'm more confused than ever. I'm not back at my bed like I would be in the Overworld. I'm somewhere completely different—and scary.

My only hope is to find my original portal and get out of this crazy place.

I'm an explorer. That's why I love this game. But it's also kind of frustrating at times. All I want to do is find new resources, create new structures, and discover new ways to use my tools. Why does that have to be so dangerous?

I guess it's no different from the real world. There are so many things to discover. But often I have no way of knowing which ones are dangerous and which ones will really help me. It's a good thing we have a God who cares about us. He has given us so many tools to help us in every situation. We have His Word, His church, and our own personal relationship with Him to rely on. If we follow His guidance, He will lead us through the dangers of our own Nether.

GAMEPLAY SECRETS

The Nether is a scary dimension filled with danger and destruction. Floating blocks of netherrack, lava falls, creepy mobs (like blazes and ghasts)...and the only way in and out is through a portal.

REAL-LIFE SECRETS

Read It

"God loved the people of this world so much that he gave his only Son, so that everyone who has faith in him will have eternal life and never really die. God did not send his Son into the world to condemn its people. He sent him to save them! No one who has faith in God's Son will be condemned. But everyone who doesn't have faith in him has already been condemned for not having faith in God's only Son" (John 3:16-18).

Think It

How do we have eternal life with God? What happens to people who don't have faith in Jesus? What did God send His Son into the world to do?

Live It

We don't like talking about it, yet the Bible makes five things clear about the place reserved for Satan, otherwise known as hell: (1) it is a real place, (2) it includes eternal separation from God, (3) God gives you and me a way to avoid it, (4) it is reality for those who do not trust the Savior, and (5) it is *not* reality for Christians—people who have committed their lives to Jesus Christ. Through Jesus, our sins are completely forgiven. Our slate is clean. We have a spotless record with Him and can now have eternal fellowship with God. "Christ also suffered once for sins, the righteous for the unrighteous, to bring you to God" (1 Peter 3:18 NIV).

Jot a Thought or Dream Up a Minecrafty Masterpiece

SECRET 34

Uses for Netherrack

I'm building a fireplace that will make my Grandma Bonnie proud.

She's a strong pioneer woman who grew up in the mountains of West Virginia, so she knows a thing or two about lighting a fire in everything from a potbellied woodstove in the kitchen to a cozy, crackling fireplace in the living room.

Her fuel of choice is coal. For me, it's netherrack.

First, I decide the best location for my fireplace—definitely in Mount Quack's great room. Then I get busy knocking out a big hole in an outside wall. I take out wooden blocks on the floor too. (I don't want my house to catch on fire.)

Next, I fill the area with brick, adding it to the firebox, the flue, the hearth, and the mantle. And finally, the fun part—placing netherrack in the firebox. Once lit, this block burns forever. And it's beautiful.

CLICK. CLICK. CLICK.

I tap my mouse and pan around the room, admiring the place.

I can't stop thinking about Grandma Bonnie. I imagine her sitting in a big chair next to the fire, sipping hot chocolate and telling funny stories about her childhood. Nearly every time, she turns the conversation to her love for Jesus and His love for us. "He's our protector," she tells me. "Our names are written in the book of life. And one day we will be with Him in heaven, shining like the stars—brighter than a crackling fire!"

I love this room so much. I especially love who it reminds me of.

"Time to add fireplaces and netherrack all over my house," I tell myself. "Yep, Grandma would be proud."

GAMEPLAY SECRETS

Netherrack is only found in the Nether. These blocks can break extremely easily, even with bare hands. When it's lit, it burns indefinitely.

Dragee90's Best Tip

I use Netherrack in fireplaces and torches.

REAL-LIFE SECRETS

Read It

"Michael, the chief of the angels, is the protector of your people, and he will come at a time of terrible suffering, the worst in all of history. And your people who have their names written in The Book will be protected. Many of those who lie dead in the ground will rise from death. Some of them will be given eternal life, and others will receive nothing but eternal shame and disgrace. Everyone who has been wise will shine as bright as the sky above, and everyone who has led others to please God will shine like the stars" (Daniel 12:1-3).

Think It

What does it mean to have our names written in The Book? (Hint: Flip back to Secret 33 and reread John 3:16-18.) Who will shine as bright as the sky above? (Please explain.)

Live It

Here's something my grandma once taught me. She explained that we can't earn our way into heaven—it just can't be done. Nothing we do, including "good" works, can protect us from the burning flame of God's holiness. "All our righteous acts are like filthy rags; we all shrivel up like a leaf, and like the wind our sins sweep us away" (Isaiah 64:6 NIV). So how can we be wise and have our names written in The Book, as Daniel says, and "shine as bright as the sky above"? Trust Christ and what He accomplished by His death and resurrection. This is the one true path to eternity. And as Christ-followers, we must tell others about Jesus so they can learn to follow Him too.

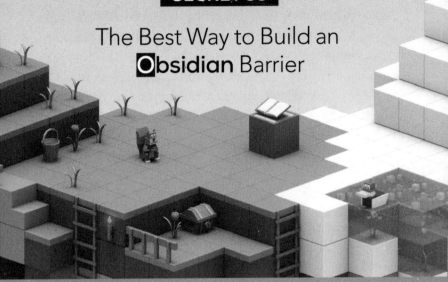

SECRET 35

The Best Way to Build an Obsidian Barrier

bsidian is blast-proof, which makes it a perfect shield against creepers.

For as long as I've played this game, I've been taunted and threatened by these creepy green dudes. You know what happens if you get too close to one—*SSSSS*...followed by *KABOOM!*

Up to this point, I've used obsidian to construct a bunker and a portal. Today, I'm making something very simple: a fireproof creeper barrier.

It all begins with a trip to my mine—level 11 or below, to be exact. That's where I can find obsidian. Once I harvest several blocks using my diamond pickaxe, I head back to the surface. And then I go to work constructing my creeper barriers—several walls just three blocks high and three blocks deep. I place them all throughout Mount Quack, both inside my house and at various strategic locations outside. Each barrier will give me a place to dive behind seconds before a creeper explodes.

As I test the barriers—running around my house and doing several tuck-and-roll moves behind my obsidian walls—my mind flashes to smoke jumpers I've met in Southern California.

These brave men and women leap out of airplanes and battle forest fires. Without their white jumpsuits—made of lightweight, fire-retardant materials that protect them from the flames and reflect the heat away from their bodies—they'd never be able to get past the first blast of heat. The jumpers must be completely covered or they can be badly burned—even killed.

I may not be wearing a creeper-proof jumpsuit, but I do have my obsidian barriers. And just in time too. As I head down a dark hall that leads to my mine, I hear that familiar warning...*SSSSS!* I take cover. *KABOOM!*

I peek around the wall and fire an arrow. *POOF!* The monster disappears, and the coast is clear again. My creeper-proof barrier works!

GAMEPLAY SECRETS

Obsidian is a purplish-blackish block that is hard to destroy. It's formed when flowing water hits lava blocks. Players spawn onto a group of these blocks when they enter the End biome. Then they mine these blocks to build towers and barriers.

Dragee90's Best Tip

Use obsidian to construct barriers in and around your shelter.

Read It

"If you have sinned, you should tell each other what you have done. Then you can pray for one another and be healed. The prayer of an innocent person is powerful, and it can help a lot" (James 5:16).

Think It

What must we do if we sin? Does Jesus forgive us? (Please explain.)

Live It

If we mess up, confession is how we get things right again. It means being totally honest with Jesus and telling Him we're sorry. It's the way we let go of guilt and receive the Lord's forgiveness. "If we confess our sins, he is faithful and just and will forgive us our sins and purify us from all unrighteousness" (1 John 1:9 NIV). Here's something else to think about: Just as smoke jumpers are made fireproof by their suits, we too can be protected from the deadly flames of sin. Our suit is Jesus Christ himself. "In Christ Jesus you are all children of God through faith, for all of you who were baptized into Christ have clothed yourselves with Christ" (Galatians 3:26-27 NIV). Jesus wraps us in His holiness, and when we come into God's presence we are protected. It's as if Jesus "took off the suit" and exposed Himself to the fiery heat of God's holiness and justice to take the punishment for us. Now that's *incredible* love!

What I Craft with Ore Blocks

It's crafting day in my little Minecraft world. And that means I've got to evaluate my inventory. *Where am I falling short? In what ways am I strong? Do I have enough tools? Weapons? Armor? Do I have a good supply of emeralds that I can trade with villagers?*

Once I figure out what I have and what I need, I can pair the right ore with the right crafting recipe. And then it's time to go to work creating all kinds of things. Here's how I use the ore blocks I mine:

> *coal*—burned as fuel in my furnace
>
> *iron*—smelted into ingots that I use for making pick-axes and armor
>
> *lapis lazuli*—turned into dye for sheep wool and used as decorations

gold—smelted into ingots that I use for making armor and swords

diamond—turned into armor and swords

redstone—used in torches, lighting systems, and pistons; also used to power things like levers, pressure plates, and tripwire hooks

emerald—used as currency when trading with villagers

Nether quartz—used as decorative blocks in my shelter.

In Minecraft—as in real life—I like to be busy, using my gifts and abilities. This means I might be shooting an arrow one second and then swinging a pickaxe the next. Boredom is my enemy—I simply can't sit still! So in the game (and in life) you'll find me creating, crafting, building...block by block.

GAMEPLAY SECRETS

There are eight ore blocks: coal, iron, gold, diamond, emerald, redstone, lapis lazuli, and Nether quartz. Each one has a specific use that can be used for mining and crafting tools. Most ore blocks must be smelted to be used, but some can be used right away.

Dragee90's Best Tip

Learn two things quickly: (1) the best pickaxe to mine each ore, and (2) smelting recipes. Know these things and your game will improve.

REAL-LIFE SECRETS

Read It

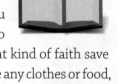

"My friends, what good is it to say you have faith, when you don't do anything to show that you really do have faith? Can that kind of faith save you? If you know someone who doesn't have any clothes or food, you shouldn't just say, 'I hope all goes well for you. I hope you will be warm and have plenty to eat.' What good is it to say this, unless you do something to help? Faith that doesn't lead us to do good deeds is all alone and dead!" (James 2:14-17).

Think It

Why is it important to do good deeds—to get busy helping others in Jesus's name? How do you serve and help others?

Live It

When Jesus says to us, "Come, follow me" (Mark 1:17 NIV), and when we do—by committing our lives to Him and following the Lord step-by-step—everything changes. Our identities, our heart's desires, how we face trouble, and how we treat others. We begin to care more about our friends and family. We want to reach out and help the world; we want our faith to be awake and active—not boring and sleepy! James 2:14-17, the Bible passage we read above, starts with two important questions: "My friends, what good is it to say you have faith, when you don't do anything to show that you really do have faith? Can that kind of faith save you?" How would you answer these questions?

SECRET 37

Tapping the Infinite Possibilities of the Overworld

I look up and gasp. The towers seem to stretch all the way to the clouds. And rising from the very tip-tops of seven red- and gray-tiled turrets—the highest points in all the land— are gold and purple crosses.

The fortress is massive with arched stained-glass windows along the sides, balconies popping out, mossy cobblestone walls, secret doors that lead to secret passageways, fountains, pools, and glassed-in gardens.

It's an Irish-Scandinavian chateau unlike any other. It's *my* chateau—Mount Quack! And to think it started as a simple shelter to protect me from the monster freak show that paraded on my doorstep each night.

I smile as I admire my world. Minecraft lets me be an artist, an engineer, an inventor, a warrior...anything I want to be. It gives me a place to dream, create, and work things out. This game is like a never-ending place of discovery.

In the real world, I feel this way whenever I think seriously about God.

My Creator is beyond my wildest imagination. He is infinite, perfect, and more powerful than any human could ever be (Hebrews 11:3). Yeah, when I focus on God I am literally awestruck! In Exodus 3:14 (NIV), God told Moses, "I AM WHO I AM" (check out Isaiah 45:5 too). He is the only real God, and He knows my name, my thoughts, my fears, and my dreams. All things are possible for Him. Even Minecraft doesn't come close to the one true source of creativity. But I'm going to continue having fun creating because it reminds me of my ultimate Creator.

TAP! TAP! TAP!

I click my mouse and open my inventory. I feel like I'm staring at an artist's palate, and the blocks are my colors. I pull out cobblestone. *Time to build something!*

GAMEPLAY SECRETS

The action begins in the Overworld. This is the starting dimension for every player, and it can generate infinitely. It consists of different biomes that may be filled with mountains, jagged cliffs, valleys, caves, deserts, beaches, oceans, jungles...seemingly endless possibilities.

Dragee90's Best Tip

Stretch your imagination and create things—castles, farms, towers, traps, secret hideaways...anything! If you don't know how, give it a try anyway. Don't be afraid to try new things.

Read It

"The LORD says: 'My thoughts and my ways are not like yours. Just as the heavens are higher than the earth, my thoughts and my ways are higher than yours'" (Isaiah 55:8-9).

Think It

What do you think God means when He says His ways are not our ways? Since God is so much smarter than us, does this mean He always knows best? (Please explain.)

Live It

The Bible tells us that God is *all-wise* and that His thoughts and ways are not like ours. In other words, He is God and we are not. He is holy and perfect. He is wiser than the smartest human who ever lived—even wiser than Solomon. Scripture says something else about God: He is *all-knowing*. There are no secrets kept from Him. To be honest, I sometimes feel a little strange imagining that God knows *all* of my thoughts. Yikes! But this, too, is actually a good thing. He isn't trying to catch me messing up. Instead, He knows me better than I do, and He knows exactly what I need. He speaks to me through my mind and emotions, through the Bible and other Christians...guiding my steps and helping me to make good choices in life. We can take comfort in the fact that our Creator is all-wise and all-knowing...and that His ways are not our ways.

Using the Right Pickaxe
for the Right Job

*S*MACK! SMACK! SMACK!

I'm in my library, slugging away on a stone staircase and on blocks of granite. I've decided to rebuild the room—expanding it and adding windows, tables, and big oversized chairs next to the bookcases. With the help of my golden pickaxe (strengthened with the Silk Touch enchantment), I'm getting the job done in the blink of an eye. "This thing's a fast, supercharged maniac," I proudly tell myself.

It's true. I'm smashing blocks in half the time I would with other pickaxes. So I turn my attention to a decorative block of lapis lazuli.

SMACK!

This time—nothing.

SMACK! SMACK! SMACK!

Still nothing.

And then right before my eyes, my pickaxe breaks, and...

POOF! It just disappears. In my mind, my duck-billed mouth drops to the ground.

What just happened?

I learned the hard way that it's important to use the right pickaxe for the right job. As with any tool in the game—and in real life—each one has a specific purpose. A flathead screwdriver doesn't work very well when the job requires a Phillips. And in Minecraft, only stone, iron, or diamond pickaxes can break a block of lapis lazuli.

Here's a handy list of what I have since learned.

Golden—A pickaxe made out of gold has the shortest life with just 33 good smacks in it (officially referred to as its *durability* and number of *uses*). But here's something to consider: It just happens to be the fastest tool, so it takes fewer smacks to break blocks of coal, redstone, brick, cobblestone, granite, quartz, and netherrack. I prefer using a golden pickaxe to break granite, quartz, and netherrack, which it can crack open in just fractions of a second. I would never attempt to try it on blocks of obsidian, diamond, emerald, iron, lapis lazuli, or (I'm embarrassed to admit I've tried this) gold.

Wooden—A pickaxe made out of wood has a short life too, with a durability of 60 uses. It's the slowest tool to work with, but it can be used to mine blocks of coal, redstone, brick, cobblestone, and granite. Only if I'm in a pinch would I try using a wooden pickaxe on quartz or netherrack...or to take out stone or weighted pressure plate. I would never use it on blocks of obsidian, diamond, gold, emerald, iron, or lapis lazuli.

Stone—A pickaxe made out of stone has a middle-of-the-road life with a durability of 132 uses. It can be used to break blocks of coal, redstone, brick, cobblestone, iron, lapis lazuli, and granite. I would never use it on blocks of obsidian, diamond, gold, or emerald.

Iron—A pickaxe made out of iron has a fairly long life with a durability of 251 uses. It's a pretty fast tool as well and can be used to break blocks of coal, diamond, emerald, redstone, brick, cobblestone, gold, iron, lapis lazuli, and granite. I prefer using an iron pickaxe to break brick, cobblestone, granite, quartz, and netherrack, which it can crack open in just fractions of a second. I would never attempt to use it on a block of obsidian.

Diamond—This is the Ferrari of pickaxes! It has the longest life of any in the game, with an unbelievable durability of 1,562 uses. It's fast and can break and harvest nearly every block in the game except an ender chest, a monster spawner, coal ore, diamond ore, emerald ore, lapis lazuli ore, Nether quartz ore, and redstone ore. A diamond pickaxe is the only one that can mine obsidian, which is how I use this tool.

GAMEPLAY SECRETS

A pickaxe is one of the most important tools in Minecraft. It's necessary to mine the ore and stone blocks, which are needed to build shelters, weapons, tools, and armor. There are various kinds of pickaxes that are needed to mine different kinds of ores. For example, a diamond pickaxe has a long life and can be used to mine just about anything.

Dragee90's Best Tip

Figure out how to use the right pickaxe for the right job. (Memorize everything I shared in today's secret.)

REAL-LIFE SECRETS

Read It

"Discover for yourself that the LORD is kind. Come to him for protection, and you will be glad. Honor the LORD! You are his special people. No one who honors the LORD will ever be in need. Young lions may go hungry or even starve, but if you trust the LORD, you will never miss out on anything good" (Psalm 34:8-10)

Think It

How does this passage make you feel, knowing that God takes care of us? (Please explain.) In what ways does God give us exactly what we need, right when we need it?

Live It

God has a purpose and a plan for each one of us. He gives us exactly what we need to accomplish His work: "No one who honors the LORD will ever be in need" (Psalm 34:9). And as you take your place in God's kingdom, you become the right person for the right job!

Three Basic Potions

C ome on, slowpoke," a voice yells through my headset. It's my gaming buddy Daffy. His character is scaling a 600-foot cliff with sheer drops to the ocean below.

"Bad idea," I respond. "There must be a better way up."

"Nope," Daffy insists. "This is it—straight up the wall. Techgirl is already waiting at the top. So start climbing!"

I'm with my friends in a stone beach biome, playing our own version of capture the flag. We're using a torch. And today, it's three against one: me, Daffy, and Techgirl versus the fastest, craziest Minecrafter in all the gaming world—the one and only Awesomecupcake. (We fondly call him Cupcake, but he wishes we'd say Awesomeness!)

Earlier, as we mined a place along the beach where lava flowed into the ocean, Cupcake spotted a tall stone tower rising high above a cliff. A burning torch flickered at the very top.

"First team to grab the torch wins," he dared us. "It's you guys against me—and I'll give you a running start."

"You're on!" Techgirl laughed as she tore through the sand and raced up the wall. Obviously someone was energized by a "Minecraft smoothie," officially known as a *potion*. I'm guessing she used the Potion of Swiftness.

Daffy and I looked at each other and then followed her. Seconds later...

"Insane," I grumble as I begin the climb.

CLICK, CLICK.

I pan down and see Cupcake several blocks below, but he's quickly gaining on me. That's when a lightbulb goes off in my duck brain. *I have my own smoothie.*

I pull out the Potion of Leaping from my hotbar and drink it. *ZING!* I suddenly have the ability to bounce up the cliff in two quick leaps. I join my friends, and together, we retrieve the torch and break into victory dabs. Cupcake groans.

In real life, my friends and I are pretty competitive. And we're intense with our faith too. We nudge each other to reach higher, to break out of our comfort zones, and to "go big" for God. We're definitely thermostats, not thermometers. (Keep reading—you'll figure out what I mean.)

"Zombies—dead ahead," Techgirl warns.

The sun is dropping, which means one puny torch isn't going to protect us from the hostile mobs that are starting to attack.

"I've got this," Cupcake says in true alpha-player fashion. (That's his inner-thermostat kicking in.) He throws a splash potion of Healing, which has an opposite effect on monsters. The zombies are stunned by the blast.

"Now run for your lives—and *fast*!" he tells us.

"I can do fast," I say. "I even have a potion for that!"

Potions are like recipes. If a player knows which ingredients to mix together, he or she can create some really cool special powers for their game. But beware...the boost each potion gives is just temporary.

Dragee90's Best Tip

Keep several different kinds of potions in your hotbar so you have what you need when you're in a tight spot.

REAL-LIFE SECRETS

Read It

"Do what the LORD your God commands and follow his teachings. Obey everything written in the Law of Moses. Then you will be a success, no matter what you do or where you go" (1 Kings 2:3).

Think It

What steps can you take to go deeper in your faith? What does the Bible say we must do in order to be successful?

Live It

Here's my best recipe for an on-fire faith.

Break your comfort zone. A comfort zone is that invisible, safe circle we put around ourselves so we don't have to be bothered by anything or anyone. It's a selfish, protective cocoon that keeps us from being all God wants us to be.

Become a thermostat, not a thermometer. A thermometer only reflects the climate around it. If the crowd is hot, the person is hot; if the crowd is cold, the person is cold. A thermostat, on the other hand, is independent. It sets the temperature and has the final say on how the climate will be. This type of believer has set his dial—and has set out to influence the surroundings.

Jot a Thought or Dream Up a Minecrafty Masterpiece

SECRET 40

How to Succeed in PVP
(Player Versus Player)

M y friends and I are playing capture the torch again, but
this time it's every Minecrafter for himself. I've got
to win. If Cupcake gets the torch first, we'll all have
to call him Awesomeness from now on. I can't let that happen!

We're in a desert biome with endless sand in every direction,
gold rabbits hopping around, villages dotting the place...and a
mysterious temple rising from the barren landscape.

Getting to the temple is my mission. That's where the torch is
hidden. But before I race into danger, I've got to check my inventory, size up my competition, and set a winning plan.

I glance at my hotbar. Weapons—*check*. Tools—*check*. Food—
check. Potions—*check*.

My competitors are extra sneaky, but I know their tactics.

Daffy will use his brains as his biggest weapon. He'll set traps,
wait patiently...and then overtake a player with the element of
surprise. Techgirl will use her spylike skills of resourcefulness.

She's able to adapt to any environment and think quickly under pressure. Above all, she'll use every potion in her arsenal for regeneration, swiftness, healing, leaping...even invisibility. As for Awesomecupcake, he'll storm the gates with brute strength. That's how he rolls. Unlike his name, his gameplay personality is intense, fearless, and intimidating.

Brains, resourcefulness, and brute strength. As for me, I think it takes a combination of all three qualities to win a game. But I usually lean toward being a ninja-warrior "brainiac"—just like my friend Daffy. And I'm sort of this way in the real world: I think through a challenge, and then I move in full-force to secure the win. But if I lose, I try to stay calm and cool.

With the clock ticking, I hide behind a dune and study the temple. Orange clay and tan sandstone blocks rise toward a cloudless blue sky. The middle of the structure looks like an ancient pyramid with steps that climb up all four sides. And smack in the front is a narrow rectangular doorway four blocks tall and three blocks wide. But it's *not* the only way in.

I wonder what kinds of surprises my friends will spring on me. Will brute strength rule the day? Will we be forced to call Cupcake "Awesomeness" from now on?

Keep reading and stay tuned...

GAMEPLAY SECRETS

PVP (player versus player) is a multiplayer competitive aspect of Minecraft in which players compete against other players. Whether working together with friends or going solo—just as we did today—this is one of the most fun and challenging ways to enjoy Minecraft.

Dragee90's Best Tip

Being properly equipped is very important whether you're entering into organized PVP or simply preparing for unexpected attacks. All this is guaranteed to take out monsters and stop players if applied effectively. Here's what you need in your arsenal: sword, bow and arrow, and flint and steel.

REAL-LIFE SECRETS

Read It

"You helped me win victories, and you forced my attackers to fall victim to me" (Psalm 18:39).

Think It

Do you like competition? (Please explain.) Good sportsmanship is important. How would God define "good sportsmanship"?

Live It

It's all about survival of the fittest, right? And the kids who survive are athletic, ruthless, and wired for one thing: crushing the competition through brute strength.

Well, not exactly. I'm competitive—and that's a good thing. But the Bible describes the best attitude to have: "You know that many runners enter a race, and only one of them wins the prize. So run to win! Athletes work hard to win a crown that cannot last, but we do it for a crown that will last forever. I don't run

without a goal. And I don't box by beating my fists in the air"
(1 Corinthians 9:24-26).

The Lord isn't impressed with shiny trophies and first-place awards. God looks at other stuff: hearts transformed by His power, eyes focused on His will, hands involved in His service. So instead of trying to clobber the competition, I do my best to make a good shot, execute a good pass, play by the rules, improve my skills, and set the right example.

Jot a Thought or Dream Up a Minecrafty Masterpiece

A **Raw Pork Chop** Can Heal a Tamed Wolf

I gently pat my wolf on the head before turning in for the night. We just crawled into a cozy igloo in the cold Taiga biome—ready to end a busy day of hunting black-and-white spotted rabbits. But seconds before closing my eyes, I hesitate.

I notice that something's not quite right with my pet wolf.

"Hey, Champ," I say with a syrupy sweet voice. "You don't look so good. Are you tired? Scared? Sick?"

Champ just blinks a few times, sticks out her tongue, and then walks around in circles. Of course, I know she can't actually hear me. Minecraft pets only respond to right clicks on our keyboards—but play along anyway. I love using my imagination!

So what's going on?

Suddenly, I notice the problem: Her tail is lower than usual, which is a sure warning that a tamed wolf's health bar is running too low. Maybe she was attacked by zombies or skeletons earlier in the day. Maybe she fell off an icy cliff while chasing rabbits.

"That's it," I say out loud. "Rabbits. Specifically, a deadly one with horizontal blood-red eyes. The infamous killer bunny!"

I'd forgotten all about these hostile mobs.

Every other rabbit we saw ran for their lives, but this one ran right toward us...threatening to end ours. That's when Champ attacked—no doubt defending me—and the two began to roll around in the snow. But after a vicious fight, Champ emerged victorious.

"You're hurt, fella," I say, patting my wolf again. "But I have just the thing that will make you as good as new."

I pull out a raw pork chop and feed it to Champ. I give her another one, and then little, bubblelike hearts begin to appear and then pop above her head. She's happy and healthy again.

If only we could tame our enemies this way, I think.

My pet was once a dangerous wolf but became a loyal friend with a little food and loving attention. Come to think of it, maybe "killing an enemy with kindness" really is the answer. But I'm not so sure it works on killer bunnies!

TAP, TAP.

I right-click on my keyboard, giving my pet the command to sit. Champ takes a spot on the floor right next to my bed.

"I love having a companion like you," I tell Champ. I lay down on my bed and drift off to sleep...imagining the kindness I can show in the real world.

GAMEPLAY SECRETS

Who doesn't like bacon...including tamed wolves? A pork chop is a food item that is obtained from pigs, which drop zero to two pieces of pork when farmed. A raw pork chop does not stack in a player's inventory. Pork can be cooked in a furnace and turned into a cooked pork chop, which increases your hunger bar.

Dragee90's Best Tip

Villager butchers will sell fourteen or so pork chops for an emerald. Above all—as you saw in today's story—a raw pork chop will heal a tamed wolf.

REAL-LIFE SECRETS

Read It

"You answered their prayers when they were in trouble. You kept your agreement and were so merciful that their enemies had pity on them. Save us, LORD God! Bring us back from among the nations. Let us celebrate and shout in praise of your holy name. LORD God of Israel, you deserve to be praised forever and ever. Let everyone say, 'Amen! Shout praises to the LORD!'" (Psalm 106:44-48).

Think It

How exactly are we to treat our enemies? How can we live in such a way that everyone—even those who don't like us—see a difference in our lives?

Live It

My dad made a comment about being a Christian that really made me think: "We may not always act so nice around others, but we should always strive to be good." *Whew!* That really takes a big weight off my shoulders. I don't like it when people are mean to me—and I'm glad I don't have to be like a human doormat. But at the same time, my dad says I can't fire back with nasty comments. I need to try to be *good*—even when others aren't being good to me.

Jesus sets the example of how we should respond: "Love your enemies, do good to those who hate you, bless those who curse you, pray for those who mistreat you." (Open your Bible and read more in Luke 6:27-31 NIV.) Just as a raw pork chop can heal a tamed wolf, in the real world, we can soothe the unkindness of others with the healing words of God. It's hard, but ask Jesus to help you do this: "Stay away from stupid and senseless arguments. These only lead to trouble, and God's servants must not be troublemakers. They must be kind to everyone, and they must be good teachers and very patient" (2 Timothy 2:23-24).

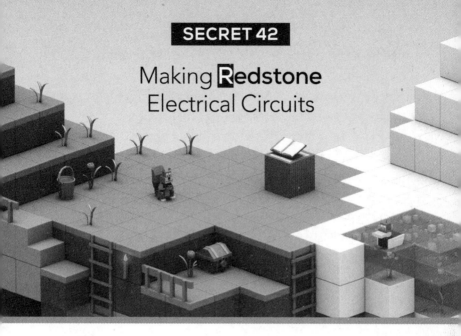

SECRET 42

Making Redstone Electrical Circuits

Today I'm playing in creative mode, experimenting with redstone.

It's mind-boggling what we can do with this ore. It can power a piston that can move multiple blocks at one time. Or it can be used in more complicated mechanical systems, like elevators, trapdoors, TNT cannons, arrow launchers, and so many other cool things...to be totally honest, things that are *way* out of my league. This is super brainy stuff.

So I'm starting with the basics. I'm making a simple redstone circuit that will power a piston. In other words, I'm building a block mover.

Step 1. Mine some redstone. You'll find tons of it in levels 1 through 16.

Step 2. Strike the redstone with an iron, gold, or diamond pickaxe to create redstone dust.

Step 3. Place the dust in a line between the piston (that you make earlier) and your power source to create a circuit. You can only place the dust on top of blocks, not on the sides. Possible power sources include redstone torches, levers, tripwire hooks, and trapped chests, among other things.

Step 4. If you need to run your circuit of redstone dust farther than 15 blocks, you will need to add a repeater (a combination of redstone dust, a redstone torch, and stone).

Step 5. Once all these items are connected, you will have a working piston that can move up to 12 blocks forward at one time. If I want to be able to move the blocks both forward and backward, I'll need to make a sticky piston. But I'll save that for another day.

BUZZ...ZAP...BOOM! Now I can work superfast and make Mount Quack even bigger and stronger. This is just the beginning.

GAMEPLAY SECRETS

Redstone is like an electric power cord. It's a conductive mineral found deep underground. When mined, it can be used to make electrical circuits and complicated mechanical systems, like elevators, trapdoors, TNT cannons, arrow launchers, and so many other things.

Dragee90's Best Tip

Redstone dust can transmit an electric current that powers stuff. It can open up so many possibilities in the game. Don't be afraid to experiment with it.

REAL-LIFE SECRETS

Read It

"May our barns be filled with all kinds of crops. May our fields be covered with sheep by the thousands, and every cow have calves. Don't let our city be captured or any of us be taken away, and don't let cries of sorrow be heard in our streets. Our LORD and our God, you give these blessings to all who worship you" (Psalm 144:13-15).

Think It

What does it mean to be blessed by God? In what ways has the Lord blessed you? Why is it hard to count our blessings when life is hard?

Live It

Regardless of our circumstances—through happy times and sad ones, troubles and victories—God wants us to make the most of every situation. The key? Remember whom you belong to:

> God, being rich in mercy, because of the great love with which he loved us, even when we were dead in our trespasses, made us alive together with Christ— by grace you have been saved—and raised us up with him and seated us with him in the heavenly places in Christ Jesus, so that in the coming ages he might show the immeasurable riches of his grace in kindness toward us in Christ Jesus. For by grace you have been saved through faith. And this is not your own doing; it is the gift of God (Ephesians 2:4-8 ESV).

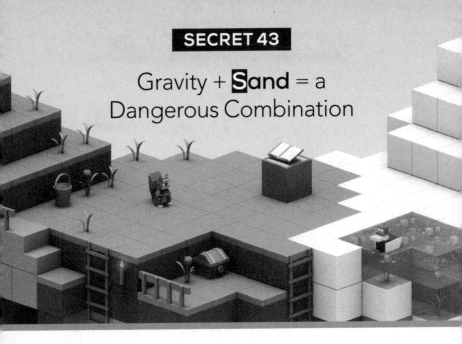

SECRET 43

Gravity + **S**and = a Dangerous Combination

I'm trapped—with sand pouring in all around me. "Got to think fast, or I'll be buried alive," I tell myself.

I'm in a spooky chamber below a desert temple.

One second, I was closing in, about to become the victor of capture the torch. But before I could get my hands on the prize, the ground gave way right under my feet. I tumbled helplessly, and then...*BOING!*

I landed on sticky cobwebs. And just as I was coming to my senses...*RRRIIIIP!* I fell again. But this time I landed with a mind-numbing *THUD.*

That's when the sand began to rain on me.

"Daffy is behind this," I tell myself. "This is exactly the kind of trap he'd dream up."

My friend is the brains behind the game—and we're on his server—so I'm positive he dug this pit long before he challenged us to a game. He's sneaky like that.

I look up. *How can I get out of this jam?* There isn't a thing I can grab onto. So is this it—game over for Dragee90?

Not a chance. I'm sneaky too. Actually, a better word would be *resourceful*—just like Techgirl. And in real life, I'd describe myself as energetic, alive, and on fire with a never-give-up attitude. That's how I live my life, my faith.

As the sand continues to pour on my head, I tap on my hotbar and retrieve my last, best hope: my one and only ender pearl. I was saving it for a rainy day...and right now it's raining sand.

Suddenly...*POOF!*

I instantly teleport to the very spot where I stepped into the trap. I retrace my steps backward and quickly retreat from the temple.

Once outside, I come face-to-bill with my competition. Awesomecupcake steps directly in front of me and raises the torch high over his head.

"Go on," he says. "Say it..."

I can hardly spit out the words. "Congratulations...*gulp*... Awesomeness!"

Daffy and Techgirl laugh hysterically through their headsets. *Now it's game over.*

GAMEPLAY SECRETS

Sand is found in desert biomes or on landscapes with oceans and beaches. And as you saw in my adventure, this block is definitely affected by gravity. Four sand blocks in a crafting grid can make sandstone. Sand can also be heated in a furnace to produce glass.

Dragee90's Best Tip

If you mine a space underneath a sand block, the sand block will fall into the newly unoccupied space. So be careful when building a sand trap, since you can easily experience cave-ins...and become the victim of your own trap!

REAL-LIFE SECRETS

Read It

"I know everything you have done, and you are not cold or hot. I wish you were either one or the other. But since you are lukewarm and neither cold nor hot, I will spit you out of my mouth. You claim to be rich and successful and to have everything you need. But you don't know how bad off you are. You are pitiful, poor, blind, and naked" (Revelation 3:15-17).

Think It

What does it mean to be lukewarm? Why do you think this upsets God?

Live It

Today's Bible passage kind of scares me. I don't want my faith to be lukewarm...and I certainly don't want God to spit me out of His mouth! I want to be growing, thriving...and crazy excited for God! So here's what my church group is doing to keep our faith alive: We're learning what it means to worship Jesus. Read John 4:1-26 for some clues. (Hint: God seeks the kind of believer who worships Him in spirit and in truth.) Remember what Jesus offers. (Here's another hint: living water.) If you're like most Christians, your faith can get pretty dry at times—as dry as sand. But the living water Jesus gives can transform the most desolate, desertlike soul into an abundant life spring!

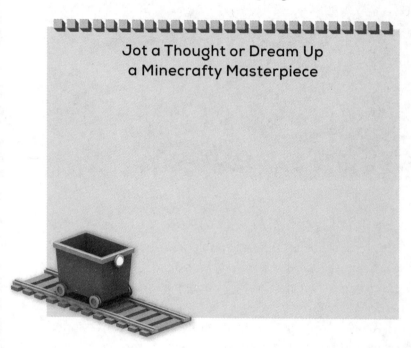

Jot a Thought or Dream Up a Minecrafty Masterpiece

SECRET 44

What to Do with Sandstone

S MACK! PLOP! CRUNCH!

It's tedious work stacking blocks in the scorching desert sun—even in a cyber world with a make-believe sun and temperatures that exist only in your mind!

SMACK! PLOP!

Another block in place, another row complete. I'm stacking layers of chiseled sandstone and chiseled red sandstone, forming a big 20-by-20 block foundation.

Next, I move upward with my layers, this time mixing in smooth sandstone and red sandstone slabs. When I pan out and inspect my work from a distance, I'm amazed. My structure is quickly taking shape.

It rises from the barren desert sand with sort of a steplike pattern. I use fewer blocks on each new level until the whole thing comes to a point with a single block at the very top. The reddish sandstone really pops, and the textured sides make the creation look incredibly old.

"A pharaoh would definitely call this home," I tell myself. "Well, a dead one anyway."

Have you figured out what I'm building? If you said a hotel for mummies, you'd be 100 percent correct. But my pyramid is going to serve as a vacation retreat for the living.

I plan to carve out a secret house inside—complete with a bedroom, a library, and a game room. I'll dig a hidden passageway to a mine below so I can gather all kinds of important resources. This will become Mount Quack South. But to villagers and desert travelers, it'll look like another ancient temple that was abandoned long, long ago.

Nobody will know what's really hidden inside.

As I continue to stack more blocks, I can't help thinking about a very different structure. Strangely enough, my thoughts turn to our first president, General George Washington, and the beautiful home he built—Mount Vernon. At first glance, his place looks like an expensive mansion constructed entirely out of sandstone blocks. Yet the place is made entirely out of yellow pine, which is obviously wood, not stone. Boards used for siding were cut to look like blocks, and then each one was *rusticated*—which means they were covered with a mixture of paint and sand. This gives the outside of Washington's house a rough, stonelike texture.

My desert pyramid tricks the eye too. Others will think of it as a tomb filled with mummies, but it will be a secret hangout for my friends and me.

GAMEPLAY SECRETS

Sandstone is made by crafting four sand blocks in a crafting grid. This block retains the look of sand while making it more durable, and it will not fall like a regular sand block.

Dragee90's Best Tip

Stairs, walls, and the outsides of buildings are great uses for sandstone.

REAL-LIFE SECRETS

Read It

"Israel, you grew fat and rebelled against God, your Creator; you rejected the Mighty Rock, your only place of safety. You made God jealous and angry by worshiping disgusting idols and foreign gods" (Deuteronomy 32:15-16).

Think It

What happens when people push God away and focus on things of this world? Does this make the Lord angry? (Please explain.) How can we separate lies from truth?

Live It

I'm slowly starting to get how appearances can be deceiving—in advertising, religion, politics, friendships...even with building materials! So this is why I'm trying to practice three words my dad likes to preach: "Learn to discern." Whether it's a product someone's trying to sell me or an idea they're passing off as Christian, I shouldn't accept things at face value. I need to engage my brain and question what's set before me. And when it comes to figuring out what's right or wrong, what's true and untrue, God's Word sets the standard.

> Finally, my friends, keep your minds on whatever is true, pure, right, holy, friendly, and proper. Don't ever stop thinking about what is truly worthwhile and worthy of praise. You know the teachings I gave you, and you know what you heard me say and saw me do. So follow my example. And God, who gives peace, will be with you (Philippians 4:8-9).

Jot a Thought or Dream Up a Minecrafty Masterpiece

From **S**apling to Giant in Two Easy Steps

My desert hideaway is missing something. Trees.

Of course, we *are* smack in the middle of a sandy, barren landscape, so these things aren't exactly abundant here.

Yet I can't help imagining how beautiful they would be. I envision my giant pyramid rising out of an oasis of jungle and acacia trees. Eventually, I'll add fountains and a pool, and I'll turn Mount Quack South into the perfect vacation spot. (Maybe I'll head here whenever the winters are bad in the real world!)

In order to plant my oasis, I'll need to gather saplings from other biomes. Next, I'll need to lay down grass blocks so the trees will have the soil they need to take root in. They'll need plenty of light too, which isn't a problem in the desert. After that, I can grow my trees from saplings to giants with just two easy steps:

Give them plenty of room to grow. Jungle saplings need five spaces above, and acacias need six.

Give them bone meal to give them a good kick. This will speed up the growth process.

Room and nourishment—that's also what "human saplings" need in the real world, right? In order to grow up, kids like you and me need plenty of space to learn, think, dream, and spread our wings. And we need nourishment from our parents, our teachers, our church. And of course we need plenty of physical food in addition to the spiritual kind. "I am the vine, and you are the branches. If you stay joined to me, and I stay joined to you, then you will produce lots of fruit. But you cannot do anything without me" (John 15:5).

I swing my iron pickaxe and begin to break up the sand blocks outside my pyramid. I have lots of work ahead of me, but I can't wait to see everything grow. Soon I'll have a true oasis in the desert. It will be fun watching my tiny trees spring up from saplings to impressive giants.

GAMEPLAY SECRETS

Six kinds of saplings can be planted: oak, birch, spruce, jungle, acacia, and dark oak. Just as I'm doing to speed up the growth of my future desert oasis, players can use bone meal to give saplings a boost, especially in places where there isn't sufficient light. Saplings have two growth stages before they grow into mature trees. They are obtained by destroying the leaves on a tree or by waiting for leaves to decay after chopping down a tree.

Dragee90's Best Tip

Saplings can be planted anywhere as long as it's on grass, but they need lots of light and room to grow or they will stay a sapling forever. Destroying a planted sapling will give it back to the player.

REAL-LIFE SECRETS

Read It

"Don't let anyone make fun of you, just because you are young. Set an example for other followers by what you say and do, as well as by your love, faith, and purity" (1 Timothy 4:12).

Think It

Do we have to be all grown up to serve God? (Please explain your answer.) In what ways is God using you to love and encourage others?

Live It

I love today's verse! We don't have to wait until we're grown up to serve God. Our generation—you and me—can touch the world with the gospel...right now, just as we are! We don't have to be Bible scholars or perfect saints to do God's work. If we're available, sincere about following Him, and teachable, He's ready to use us. "Now go! When you speak, I will be with you and give you the words to say" (Exodus 4:12).

What kinds of things can we do to serve God? Jesus gives

some great ideas in Matthew 25:31-46. Activities like feeding the hungry, clothing the naked, taking care of the sick, visiting people in prison. Collect old blankets from neighbors and hand them out to homeless families in your town. All around you are people in need of a friend. Your school campus is a great place to start. Help someone who is hurting. Hey, here's an idea: Start a campus Bible study.

Jot a Thought or Dream Up a Minecrafty Masterpiece

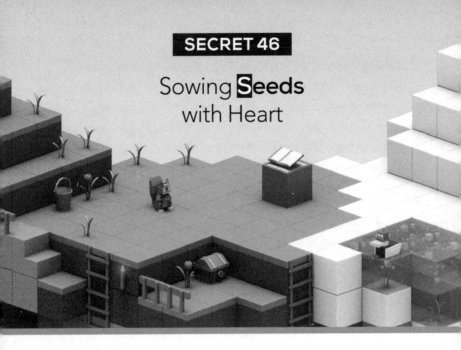

SECRET 46

Sowing Seeds
with Heart

As I break up tall grass and collect its seeds, I get excited thinking about the five crops I'm going to grow at my farm:

Melons—a fruit that makes my mouth water.

Pumpkins—a primary ingredient in pie. (But it must include whipped cream.)

Potatoes—a favorite, as long as they speak French.

Carrots—a way to entice rabbits, which ultimately become stew.

Wheat—a first step toward becoming a Minecraft farmer.

So here I am in a field of tall grass, gathering wheat seeds. Once I've scooped up the last ones—by walking over them, of course—I'll need to craft a wooden hoe with sticks.

Next, I stake out a patch of land that will become my farm, and then I use my hoe on the dirt blocks. As I till them, they turn into farmland blocks.

Finally...*TAP, TAP.* I right-click on the soil blocks to plant my seeds, and then I pour a bucket of water over everything. I wait for a while, and then the seeds begin to grow into wheat plants. I've now graduated from the Minecraft School of Farming, and I'm ready to grow anything. It's that easy!

I wonder if my great-great-grandfather would agree? Probably not. He came to America from Sweden to farm the fertile landscapes of Wisconsin and Nebraska. And my great-grandfather carried on that tradition in Idaho. They worked extremely hard, carving out a living from the land. My grandpa decided to be a painter instead, and my dad is a writer. But an even greater legacy continues with me—planting seeds of faith.

Using my hoe, I till more dirt blocks. I sow seeds with heart, proud of my farming heritage. Soon I'll have gardens overflowing with melons, pumpkins, potatoes, carrots, and wheat.

But I can't stop here. What's a farm without chickens, cows, and pigs? Mount Quack is destined to be the farming center of the Jungle M biome!

GAMEPLAY SECRETS

Seeds are planted on tilled grass blocks, using a hoe. In order for them to grow, the grass block must have a water source next to it. Otherwise, everything will dry up and die. Most seeds are acquired by tilling grass or dirt blocks.

Dragee90's Best Tip

Use your pickaxe to cut out several strips of blocks, separated by a row of dirt blocks. Above all, kick-start the growth of seeds with water and bone meal.

REAL-LIFE SECRETS

Read It

"Now listen! A farmer went out to scatter seed in a field. While the farmer was scattering the seed, some of it fell along the road and was eaten by birds. Other seeds fell on thin, rocky ground and quickly started growing because the soil wasn't very deep. But when the sun came up, the plants were scorched and dried up, because they did not have enough roots. Some other seeds fell where thornbushes grew up and choked out the plants. So they did not produce any grain. But a few seeds did fall on good ground where the plants grew and produced thirty or sixty or even a hundred times as much as was scattered" (Mark 4:3-8).

Think It

What helped some of the seeds to grow? When it comes to growing our faith, what kind of soil do we need? (Please explain.) What does God want to grow in our lives? (For some clues, open your Bible and read Galatians 5:22-23.)

Live It

The Bible teaches that there are four kinds of spiritual soil: *the hard path* (when faith doesn't take root and fades away), *rocky places* (when faith is shallow), *thorns* (when faith is weighed down by worry), and *good soil* (when faith has deep, healthy roots and is growing strong). Of course, planting our faith in the good spiritual soil is our goal. Kids who do this have heard God's Word and believe it. They are committed to letting God cultivate all kinds of healthy stuff in them, especially the fruit of the Spirit: "God's Spirit makes us loving, happy, peaceful, patient, kind, good, faithful, gentle, and self-controlled. There is no law against behaving in any of these ways" (Galatians 5:22-23).

Jot a Thought or Dream Up a Minecrafty Masterpiece

Skeletons Burn in the Light

CLICK-CLACK!

"It's getting closer," I tell myself.

CLICK-CLACK!

I'm alone in the dark, scrunched between my bed and my chest. I can hear the clickety-clack of bony feet on my cobblestone floor. Each step begins at the entrance of my mine and continues down a long hallway. *CLICK-CLACK! CLICK-CLACK!*

But just as it reaches my bedroom...*CRUNCH!* After that, I hear the sweetest sound of all...*silence.* "Awesome!" I whisper to myself. "My skeleton trap is keeping me safe."

Why am I trying to catch these rattlin' rascals?

Lately, as nightfall invades gameplay, skeletons have been climbing out of my mineshaft like nasty cockroaches popping out of a drain. Hordes of them scamper down the dimly lit corridors of Mount Quack, their bows raised and ready. And they always march in one direction—right toward *me*! Before I have a second to think...*WHOOSH!* Arrows are flying past my head, and I'm running for my life.

Since it's one against dozens, I'm determined to outsmart them. A well-placed trap is the answer. So earlier, I knocked out some cobblestone and dug a pit—right outside my bedroom. The idea is to contain them during the night. In the morning, I'll just sit back and let the sun finish the job. Skeletons catch fire in the sunlight.

Will my plan work?

I asked that same question in real life as I stood before the head custodian at school, asking if he'd kindly retrieve an expensive basketball. (It was a gift from my uncle, so I didn't want to lose it.) I was at basketball practice with the guys, and to be honest, we were messing around a lot—playing dodgeball instead of shooting hoops. The coach *and* the custodian chewed us out several times.

So what happened? When they weren't in the gym we horsed around some more, and my basketball got stuck behind a bleacher. I knew what I had to do: confess what had happened. The coach made me apologize to a very agitated custodian. After I had endured some embarrassment, he eventually retrieved my basketball.

Back at Mount Quack, the first rays of sunlight are shining through stained-glass windows that line my corridor.

"Hope my trap is empty," I tell myself. "Hope the sun eliminated my monster infestation." I slowly move toward the opening of the pit and glance inside.

Suddenly...*WHOOSH!*

Arrows race past my head, and I jump back just in time. *How is that possible?*

I quickly spot the problem: I made the pit too deep, so the sun's rays can't flood the trap. And there isn't enough light in the hallway. Time to get to work, making the opening larger and knocking a hole in my roof. "I've always wanted a skylight," I tell myself. "But there's no messing around today. I have to get the job done before nightfall."

Never a dull moment in the game—and in life!

GAMEPLAY SECRETS

Skeletons are aggressive mobs that spawn in dark places or at night. They're very good shots with a bow, but not to worry—they burn in sunlight when it hits them.

Dragee90's Best Tip

If an army of deadly skeletons are attacking your house, trap them and then hold out until morning. The sun will take care of them for you.

REAL-LIFE SECRETS

Read It

"Don't take part in doing those worthless things that are done in the dark. Instead, show how wrong they are. It is disgusting even to talk about what is done in the dark. But the light will show what these things are really like. Light shows up everything, just as the

Scriptures say, 'Wake up from your sleep and rise from death. Then Christ will shine on you'" (Ephesians 5:11-14).

Think It

What are some "worthless things" that Christians should never take part in? (Take a look at Ephesians 5:3-5 for some clues.) What happens when Christ's light shines on us?

Live It

Okay...we've gotten to know each other a little better. (You saw what happened during practice.) So now I'm ready to share another bad choice I made—this one in secret, which eventually went public. It caused *lots* of embarrassment...again! Here's what happened.

Mom and Dad let me invite a couple of friends over for a sleepover. At first, the night was great. My buddies and I had fun...scarfing snacks, drinking sodas, playing video games, and just hanging out.

But as it got late, things got crazy. We snuck outside after curfew and explored a trail behind our house while another buddy recorded our moonlight adventure. And then he posted it online. All our parents found out, and yes, we were in big trouble. It was a dumb thing to do, and I felt really bad for disobeying my parents. Moral of the story: Just as skeletons burn in the light, God's kids should never take part in "doing those worthless things that are done in the dark." (In Secret 49, I'll offer some ideas on how to stay out of trouble.)

SECRET 48

Protecting Your **S**kin

I f you spend much time in multiplayer, you can't help but notice all the different custom skins in the game. Of course by *skins* I mean the countless character options that are available to download, as well as the ones players create themselves. These become our personalized Minecraft identities, and they're definitely a fun part of gameplay.

For example, I'm a duck...and so is my friend Daffy. You've met my other buddy, Awesomecupcake. He's a football player and even wears Minnesota Vikings colors! Techgirl decided to be her favorite real-world, black-and-white tabby cat.

The sky's the limit on what you can be in the game. I've seen superheroes (Batman, Wonder Woman, and Ironman), presidents (Washington, Lincoln, and Roosevelt), celebrities (Jennifer Lawrence, Nick Jonas, and Johnny Depp as Jack Sparrow), Star Wars characters, *Hobbit* creatures, and just about every kind of animal you can imagine—from creepy to cuddly.

Just as in real life, it's important to protect our skin...but I don't mean with hats and sunblock. I'm talking about safety and survival. Here are four things I do.

Find shelter. It's our first mission in Minecraft, right? But I also find shelter through trustworthy friends—guys and girls who don't act like griefers.

Avoid darkness. A simple torch can help. It'll keep the creepy-crawlies away and can guide our path through dangerous mineshafts and lonely landscapes. (Can you think of another kind of "torch" that helps this way?)

Ramp up my hotbar. I like to keep everything I need right at my fingertips. So I organize my hotbar with weapons, tools, blocks, food, potions...you name it. I protect my skin by staying smart and prepared.

Maximize my tools, It's important to have a good selection of pickaxes—stone, iron, gold, and diamond. I also craft an axe, a hoe, a shovel, and a sword. Exercising our brains, tapping into our talents, and using the right tool for the right job...these are keys to a successful Minecrafty life!

GAMEPLAY SECRETS

In Minecraft, *skin* means *character*. In the PC edition of the game, players begin with Steve (a male character) and Alex (a female character). The Console Edition of the game has eight default skin and outfit (clothing) options for Steve and eight for Alex. Outfit options include tennis, tuxedo, athlete, default, Swedish, cyclist, prisoner, and boxer. Also, players can choose *skin packs* (in various Minecraft editions) that provide a wide range of customizable kits. For example, you'll find Biome Settlers Pack 1 Skin Pack, Minecraft Story Mode Skin Pack, and Redstone Specialists Skin Pack...just to name a few. And of course, players can customize their identities for gameplay, just as I did. I'm a warrior duck with yellow and orange feathers. You can be just about anything!

Dragee90's Best Tip

Buying skin packs and downloading them can get costly *and* risky. The Internet is filled with businesses that sell Minecraft skins. Some can't be trusted because they feature inappropriate characters. My suggestion: Get your parents' help.

REAL-LIFE SECRETS

Read It

"God planned for us to do good things and to live as he has always wanted us to live. That's why he sent Christ to make us what we are" (Ephesians 2:10).

Think It

Do you like the kid God created you to be? (Why or why not?) What are some gifts and abilities He has given you?

Live It

Sometime soon, stand in front of a full-length mirror and evaluate the person you see. As you study the kid in the mirror, ask yourself some honest questions: *Who am I? Who does God say I am? How can I become more confident? How is Jesus going to change me? What must I accept about myself?* Next, talk to God. Ask Him to help you make the most of what you have. Try to improve the things that are within your power to change, and accept what you cannot change. And then remind yourself of two awesome truths:

"If God is on our side, can anyone be against us?" (Romans 8:31).

"Christ gives me the strength to face anything" (Philippians 4:13).

**Jot a Thought or Dream Up
a Minecrafty Masterpiece**

SECRET 49

Don't Get Bumped by Slime

SLAP! SLAP! SLOOOSH!

"There it is again," I tell myself. "That strange slapping sound." I raise my golden sword and stand motionless. I hardly take a breath.

SLAP! SLOOOSH!

I'm several blocks underground, mining gold in a dimly lit cavern—and my hard work is really paying off today. As I slug away on the cave walls, rich veins of the precious ore crack open right before my eyes. But that strange noise— *SLAP! SLOOOSH!*

What is it? And why can't I see it?

SLAP! SLOOOSH!

Suddenly, I get my wish. On the far end of the cavern I spot several green, Jell-O-like creatures hopping around like crazy. Some are tiny, and others are quite big. And each one is in the shape of a translucent cube. I can't help laughing. They're just bunched up in the corner, wobbling and twitching...and then randomly bouncing into the air.

Now what harm can these guys cause?

My thoughts hop back to the real world. *"It's totally okay,"* a friend says. *"Nobody will find out—and it's not like it's going to hurt you."* Famous last words, right? If a buddy says something like this—trying to convince you that a clearly wrong choice is actually right—well, you know what to do: Run from trouble.

Something tells me that's exactly what I should do right now.

The larger creature hops right up to me and begins bumping into me. "Slime!" I yell. "Gross!"

It bumps me again and again. I strike it with my sword...and then *SLOOOSH!* It multiplies into smaller cubes, which also begin to slime me. Before I know it, they're coming at me from every direction.

"Okay—it's time to do what any smart duck would do," I tell myself. "It's time to get my feet moving...and *run!*"

GAMEPLAY SECRETS

Slime is a hostile mob that spawns underground and in swampy landscapes. And watch out: Slime is as nasty as it sounds. It moves around by hopping, and if it spots you, it'll jump on you to take you down.

 ### Dragee90's Best Tip

Since slimes can see you through solid blocks, they begin to attack before you even realize you're "mob prey." Listen for the slapping noise they make and lead them to either lava or a cliff—they'll take the bait just about every time. Or do what I did—run for your life.

REAL-LIFE SECRETS

Read It

"They have turned against the LORD and can't be trusted. They have refused his teaching and have said to his messengers and prophets:

> Don't tell us what God has shown you and don't preach the truth. Just say what we want to hear, even if it's false. Stop telling us what God has said! We don't want to hear any more about the holy God of Israel.

"Now this is the answer of the holy God of Israel: 'You rejected my message, and you trust in violence and lies. This sin is like a crack that makes a high wall quickly crumble and shatter like a crushed bowl. There's not a piece left big enough to carry hot coals or to dip out water.'

"The holy LORD God of Israel had told all of you, 'I will keep you safe if you turn back to me and calm down. I will make you strong if you quietly trust me'" (Isaiah 30:9-15).

Think It

What are some slimy, bad choices that friends sometimes make? What can we do to avoid getting slimed?

Live It

There are consequences for hanging out with friends who constantly get into trouble. They usually include misery—for you, for them, for everyone. Sometimes friends will try anything to be liked. So they make a stupid choice once, then twice...and before they know it—*ssslip*—they're heading over the edge and right into trouble. Maybe it's cheating, lying, or stealing. Believe me, it's smart to avoid the trouble. How? My parents taught me three steps that really work.

Make a game plan. Decide ahead of time why and how you're going to say no to bad choices.

Sever bad ties so you don't get tied up. It's hard, but sometimes we have to end friendships with kids who gravitate toward trouble.

Consider the consequences. Think about how a choice might impact your friendship with God, your plans, your family, and your future.

Jot a Thought or Dream Up a Minecrafty Masterpiece

SECRET 50

Amazing **S**melting Techniques

It's smelting day in my world—and so, once again, I feel like a one-man machine. I add fuel to my furnace, plop in the right ingredients...and *BOOM!* Out comes something new and useful for the game.

That's what smelting is all about. Here's how I do it:

Cooking food. This is my chance to be a chef and put my Food Network skills to work. Well, sort of. Cooking is pretty basic in Minecraft. (No fancy mascarpone-filled pastas or ambrosia salads.) It all begins with a raw ingredient (the *input* block)—maybe a pork chop, a piece of chicken meat, or a potato. Heat it in your furnace, and before you know it, dinner is served. (An *output* block appears in the furnace grid.)

Turning ores and materials into useful stuff. I smelt seven items in my furnace: iron ore, gold ore, sand cobblestone, netherrack, clay, and stone bricks. I often turn a chunk of gold ore into a gold ingot—which I then use to mold weapons and armor. And I definitely turn sand into glass—which becomes windows, stained glass, and bottles.

At home in the real world, I love heating up my favorite brand of macaroni and cheese. It's almost as easy as making stuff in Minecraft. I take the food out of the carton, pull back the plastic covering (to vent it), pop it in the microwave, and punch the two-minute button. Afterward, I sprinkle a little cheese on top—just to feel like a chef.

As I dive into my snack, I find myself wishing our lives could be "smelted" in the same easy way. But growing from kid to adult—and growing our faith—takes a lot of work. The changes we go through can be hard. But I know the goal is worth the effort.

Back in Minecraft, I decide to smelt some gold ore. My sword is damaged from all the action it has seen in the mines—fighting off everything from slime to zombies.

I fuel up the furnace with coal, add some ore...and wait. Once my inventory is replenished with tools, weapons, and armor, the adventure will begin all over again. It's kind of like life!

GAMEPLAY SECRETS

Smelting is a key to creating stuff in Minecraft—which includes cooking and changing items so they can be used for food or building things. It involves melting, baking, cooking, burning, drying, and changing items into something totally new. A player must add acceptable ingredients (the input) to a furnace, and a corresponding output will be given. For example, you put sand in a furnace to melt it and produce glass blocks. You can then use the glass to make things like bottles or windows.

Dragee90's Best Tip

If you think you can save time by sleeping while the furnace churns away, smelting stuff—forget it. Time pauses in Minecraft when we sleep in a bed. My advice: Designate a smelting day and resolve to put in the time to make items. You'll be glad you did, even though smelting isn't as exciting as, say, exploring.

REAL-LIFE SECRETS

Read It

"On that day you will be glad, even if you have to go through many hard trials for a while. Your faith will be like gold that has been tested in a fire. And these trials will prove that your faith is worth much more than gold that can be destroyed. They will show that you will be given praise and honor and glory when Jesus Christ returns" (1 Peter 1:6-7).

Think It

What are some trials that you and your family have had to endure? How did you survive those hardships?

Live It

"Are you serious? We're *moving*? I have to leave my friends in Nebraska and start a new school in Missouri? Why is this happening?"

At first, my parents' decision to move us from Cornhusker country to the Show Me State hit hard. I liked our life just the way it was. I didn't want to change, and I definitely didn't want to be a stranger in a strange place. I was pretty mad, and my faith was being tested.

But then something cool happened. We moved...and we survived. And life in Missouri wasn't so strange. Actually, it was really good. God was there—in the friendly people we met at church and the new friends I made at school. I'm starting to trust God's smelting techniques: "Your faith will be like gold that has been tested in a fire."

Jot a Thought or Dream Up a Minecrafty Masterpiece

SECRET 51

Soul Sand
Slows the Enemy

I've eliminated my skeleton problem at Mount Quack, but now I'm facing a creepy zombie invasion. The solution: another well-placed trap near my mineshaft.

But instead of digging a second pit, I'm knocking out some cobblestone between my bedroom and my mine, and I'm replacing the entire floor with soul sand. This stuff slows the movement of any mob—or player—that steps into it. As I add the last block, I have to be careful not to get trapped in my own trap!

When night finally hits, the green creatures pop out of my mine, right on cue.

I make sure they see me. "I'm here, boys," I taunt. "Here's a juicy duck meal, just waiting for your taste buds!" (Hmmm...I'm actually not so sure they can actually taste anything.)

AAARRROAR!

The zombies moan as they lumber toward me. Pulling a

parkour move, I run up a wall and then somersault right over the pit. I land on the other side, raise my bow...and wait.

My mind flashes to a moment in my life when I, too, got stuck in *real* sinking sand. My family and my best friend were on vacation at the Great Sand Dunes National Park in Colorado. All of us had just finished sledding down a massive dune half the size of a mountain. (No kidding!) It took us an hour to climb to the top, and less than five minutes to reach the bottom. But as we crawled off our boards and stood up—yikes! We began to sink in the moist quicksand around us. Together, we helped each other to safety and made the long trek back up the dune. I remember thinking, *This is the only way to get unstuck from anything that traps us: God and our friends.*

My thoughts return to the game as the zombies step into the soul sand—one by one—and get temporarily stuck. "Better get busy," I tell myself. The sand has merely slowed their moves. These beasts are determined to get a juicy duck meal. "Not today, boys!"

WHOOSH!

I let the arrows fly and eliminate another Minecraft challenge.

GAMEPLAY SECRETS

Soul sand is a block that's found only in the Nether. It can be mined with any tool, but a shovel is the fastest way of retrieving it. I use it exclusively for traps. As you just saw, it slows the movement of any mob or player, and it causes them to sink into the ground a bit.

Dragee90's Best Tip

Adding water and ice to soul sand enhances the sinking effect.

REAL-LIFE SECRETS

Read It

"Christ has set us free! This means we are really free. Now hold on to your freedom and don't ever become slaves of the Law again" (Galatians 5:1).

Think It

If we mess up and sin, what does the Bible tell us to do? How does Jesus set us free?

Live It

I'm thrilled about today's verse. And here's another one that makes me happy. "Sin pays off with death. But God's gift is eternal life given by Jesus Christ our Lord" (Romans 6:23). We can stop sweating and start cheering. In fact, put down this book right now and break out into a loud cheer. It's okay if people think you are crazy—this is a crazy, wonderful truth! We don't have the strength to free ourselves, but Jesus has more than enough for us. Only His blood can wash away sin and destroy its work within us. Only Jesus can break the chains that bind us and bring freedom through forgiveness and grace that will allow us to escape the wages of death. But in doing so, our "Frankenstein inside" must be put to death—along with our old selves that are chained to sin. We must become new creations in order to be completely free. And God has made a way—by being honest about our weaknesses, telling Jesus everything in prayer, and surrendering to Him.

Jot a Thought or Dream Up a Minecrafty Masterpiece

Remembering Your **S**pawn Point

I'm surrounded.

I can't go to my left, and there's an angry mob to my right. There's nothing but water behind me, and it's starting to get dark. The only chance I have is to head straight into the woods and face the unknown. So I take off as fast as I can as I dodge trees and limbs.

Oh no, what's that sound? It's a creeper. I should have known there would be creepers in these dark woods. They're everywhere. I know there are tools that could help me out of this mess, but I'm too busy trying to survive to figure out what they are. I tend to do this in my real life too.

The hissing sounds are getting louder, which means the creepers are getting closer. I make quick turns as I try to outrun them. But there are just too many. *BOOM!* They begin to explode all around me.

Suddenly, I find myself back at the spot where I first

entered this world. Yep, the creepers got me. And now I've respawned at the same place where I began this journey. But since I have begun to build a structure on this spot, I respawn at the highest point. I look around and see the beacon on my castle in the distance. It's getting darker now, and I must make a run for shelter before some other creature gets me. Why did I make it so far from where this world originally spawned? Once I make it through this adventure, I must remember to reset my spawn point. I can do this by using the */spawnpoint* command. It would be smart to reset it closer to home. But for now I must run.

My friend Awesomecupcake likes to build his shelter near the world's original spawn point. Then he can find his way home by using his compass. And he always takes time to obtain an exploration map that shows the location of mansions and monuments. These, of course, are better ways to find a spawn point. I usually find mine only after I've been killed by some crazy creature.

I should really get better at using these tools. Why do I keep doing things the hard way? I tend to do this in my life too. I don't always use the tools that will make my life better. I have a Bible, but it's hard to find the time to read it. I have Christian parents, but I don't like to ask for advice. I often wish I were wiser, but I forget to pray and ask for guidance. I need to stop doing things the hard way and spend more time using the tools I've been given. Life would be so much better.

This is the location where players first spawn in Minecraft and where they subsequently respawn if they are knocked out of action. Also, this is the location the compass points to.

Dragee90's Best Tip

This helps you to find your way around your Minecraft world when you go exploring.

REAL-LIFE SECRETS

Read It

"Children, you belong to the Lord, and you do the right thing when you obey your parents. The first commandment with a promise says, 'Obey your father and your mother, and you will have a long and happy life'" (Ephesians 6:1-3).

Think It

What are some good memories you have with your family? What are some tough ones? What can you do to help make life better on the home front?

Live It

You've probably noticed that parents don't always make sense. Minutes after they say you're not old enough to do something, they tell you to grow up and act your age. What's up with that? And it feels like worry is a part of their DNA. They're anxious when I stay at a friend's house for a sleepover. They're nervous when I ride in a car with another family.

But know what? I wouldn't want them to change a thing. Even though we don't always agree about things, God put them in charge of my life. I want to show them how much I love them by giving them my respect and obedience. The Bible says if we do this, we will have "a long and happy life."

Jot a Thought or Dream Up a Minecrafty Masterpiece

Eyes of Ender Can Locate **S**trongholds

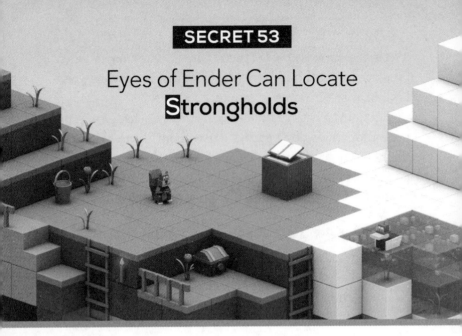

A green, glowing eye stares up at me from the palm of my hand. It's the Eye of Ender, and I can't stop looking at it. Its pupil is a narrow, black slit—like that of a snake or of a lizard. Maybe even a zombie. It's tiny, rare, and more precious than the emeralds and diamonds in my inventory.

But can it actually see stuff? And will it ever blink?

Actually, it is very much a real eye, but it can see only one thing: a stronghold. And that's why I crafted it. I've come to the Savanna M biome to find one of these rare places. The underground complexes of a stronghold are filled with long corridors, spiral staircases, mysterious chambers, ancient libraries, chests stuffed with treasure...and portals that lead to the End. Every biome has a stronghold, but they're impossible to find on our own. Only an Eye of Ender can lead us there.

I throw it into the sky, and it hovers motionless for a second, as if to seek out its prey.

Without warning...*WHOOSH!*

It begins to zip across the landscape. It flies over tall grass and acacia trees...and zooms right through blocks of red clay. I follow the trail of purple particles it leaves behind.

My mind flashes to some invisible things in the real world—things like cells in our bodies, atoms, the wind...These things are very much real, but we can't see them without the help of a microscope or the moving branches of a tree or the sense of touch.

It's that way with our faith. Fortunately, we have the Holy Spirit and the Bible to guide us. "By him all things were created, in heaven and on earth, visible and invisible, whether thrones or dominions or rulers or authorities—all things were created through him and for him" (Colossians 1:16 ESV).

Back in Minecraft, the trail from the Eye of Ender stops at the base of jagged, rocky hill. *But where's the Eye of Ender?* I look up just in time to watch it fall at my feet.

"Ender marks the spot," I say as I snatch the eye and put it back in my inventory. I pull out an iron pickaxe and begin slugging away at the ground.

GAMEPLAY SECRETS

Strongholds are structures that occur naturally underground. They're important because they house End portals. They can be located using Eyes of Ender.

Dragee90's Best Tip

A stronghold is an amazing but eerie place to explore. It contains lots of rooms—large spaces that are beautifully decorated, as well as empty rooms that feel lonely. There are scary prison cells and inviting libraries. There are staircases and corridors with chests. And of course, there's an End portal room with pools of lava, making it hard to navigate. But that's where the Eye of Ender comes in handy. Players can craft one using ender pearls.

REAL-LIFE SECRETS

Read It

"We are not fighting against humans. We are fighting against forces and authorities and against rulers of darkness and powers in the spiritual world" (Ephesians 6:12).

Think It

Do you listen to your conscience—that inner voice that warns you when something just isn't right? Do you stop and pray, and ask Jesus what to do?

Live It

Believe it or not, Christians are actually soldiers in God's army. We're fighting a big battle between good and evil...right and wrong. The devil and his troops are viciously attacking the kingdom of

God—which includes you and me! His target? Our souls. But Jesus has given us victory and has armed us with spiritual weapons packed with divine power—the sword of the spirit (the Holy Bible) and prayer. Colossians 3:16 says, "Let the message about Christ completely fill your lives," and Philippians 4:7 promises that the peace of Christ will bless you and "control the way you think and feel." In other words, as we read our Bibles and pray, God gives us the strength to do what's right and to stand up against the devil's schemes. Listen to Jesus, and you'll win the battle!

Jot a Thought or Dream Up a Minecrafty Masterpiece

Exploring Hidden Temples

C heck it out, Techgirl," I shout through my headset. "It's the lost city—Atlantis!"

My friend laughs sarcastically. "You're crazy," she says. "The *real* Atlantis is on a beach with cool waterslides and friendly dolphins. But this place? It's just weird!"

Techgirl and I are at the bottom of the Deep Ocean biome, getting ready to explore a massive underwater temple. We're floating around in our diamond armor, wearing helmets that are supercharged with the Respiration and Aqua Affinity enchantments. (These enable us to breathe underwater and work really fast.) Our blue outfits sort of remind me of scuba gear.

We swim through a large entryway and make our way inside. "Stay alert," I warn. "'Cyber Atlantis' is no amusement park!"

Like the temples in jungles and deserts, this aquatic version is filled with endless corridors, mysterious chambers, hidden treasure...and, of course, *danger*. Hey, what do you expect? This is Minecraft!

"Squid—just ahead," Techgirl warns.

"I see it."

I raise my sword, and then...*POW!* The squid drops three ink sacs that I quickly add to my inventory. "I need these for a book I'm creating," I tell Techgirl.

"No kidding," she says. "You're writing a book? *You*?"

"Funny," I say.

I look around our murky underwater world and soak up the beauty—literally! Sea lanterns add a dim glow to the rooms, and in every direction green prismarine blocks come into focus. Yellow-speckled wet sponges dangle from the ceilings overhead. As we reach the center of the monument, the passageway opens to a large room with eight gold blocks built into the wall.

"We've found the treasure chamber," Techgirl says.

"Beautiful," I respond.

My mind instantly flashes to my family's real-world vacation in the Bahamas. Every day during that trip, I couldn't help feeling that we'd landed in paradise. We explored beaches covered with white sand, and we swam in crystal-clear water. *What will our ultimate paradise be like?* I wondered. One day, I opened my Bible to find out:

> The wall was jasper, the color of Glory, and the City was pure gold, translucent as glass. The foundations of the City walls were garnished with every precious gem imaginable: the first foundation jasper, the second sapphire, the third agate, the fourth emerald (Revelation 21:18-19 MSG).

"Okay—let's get to work," Techgirl says, snapping me back to our Minecraft reality. "I'll keep watch for hostile mobs while you grab the goodies in the chests."

"Aye, Captain," I say with a laugh. "Another day in paradise!"

But just as I prepare to gather the usual loot, a hostile mob attacks.

"It's an elder guardian," Techgirl warns. "And it looks pretty vicious!"

I raise my sword again and prepare for another challenge.

So, what's an elder guardian? And can we defeat this thing? Stay tuned...

GAMEPLAY SECRETS

Whether they're underwater or above ground, ancient temples are breathtaking to look at and exciting to explore—even in Minecraft. They're filled with hidden chambers, unexpected secrets, and mysteries to unlock. Each one is unique and holds special rewards for smart players.

Dragee90's Best Tip

Don't be caught off guard by the beauty of a Minecraft temple. Stock your hotbar with weapons, tools, and food well before you enter a temple. And of course, revving up your helmet with the Respiration and Aqua Affinity enchantments are the only way to breathe and explore underwater—should you be brave enough to enter an ocean monument.

REAL-LIFE SECRETS

Read It

"There are many rooms in my Father's house. I wouldn't tell you this, unless it was true. I am going there to prepare a place for each of you. After I have done this, I will come back and take you with me. Then we will be together. You know the way to where I am going" (John 14:2-4).

Think It

What does Jesus mean when He says, "I am going there to prepare a place for each of you" in His Father's house? Will we live in houses in heaven? (For a clue, look up Isaiah 65:21).

Live It

After you read this, sit quietly for a moment, close your eyes, and try to imagine what heaven will be like. Whenever I do this, here's what I see: Lots and lots of smiling faces—those of my Christian brothers and sisters from all over the world, my family, my friends, and my Lord Jesus Christ (Isaiah 25:8-9); a big, happy celebration (Luke 13:29-30); people with perfect, strong bodies (Isaiah 35:5-6); a beautiful city of gold and crystal that's far more amazing than anything I could ever create in Minecraft (Revelation 21:18-27). Go ahead and look up the verses I included here, and then imagine what heaven will be like.

A Torch That Lights My Path

"Watch out, Dragee90," Techgirl warns through her headset. "An elder guardian is too close for comfort."

Its lone eye is fixed on me, and I know it's about to attack. The problem is, I just can't see the hostile creature. An invisible monster in a shadowy world spells trouble.

"I need my torch!" I shout, swiping my sword left and then right. "This is useless. I can't fight what I can't see. Any ideas, Techgirl?"

My friend and I are exploring an underwater temple in the Deep Ocean biome. Obviously, torches don't work down here. Sea lanterns provide our only source of light, but they are pretty wimpy as we descend deeper into the structure.

EEERRAAAKK!

I can hear the elder guardian's ghastly scream. But suddenly...

Light. Everywhere.

Techgirl pulls a jack-o'-lantern from her inventory, making

the dim underwater chamber crystal clear. The flame is protected through the carved pumpkin.

Unfortunately, though, help comes a second too late. Just as I'm about to strike...

ZZZIIITTT!...ZAP!

A purple laser stuns my body. "What just happened?" I moan.

I uttered those same words one stormy night as the lights flickered in my real-world bedroom. Suddenly, the power went out and I sat in total darkness. The next sound I heard was as ghastly as an elder guardian's scream—*EEERRAAAKK!* It was a tornado warning, which meant I had to act fast—navigating the darkness and making my way to our basement. Moments later, I felt the safe embrace of my family. We clicked on our flashlights and opened God's Word: "This is the message we have heard from him and declare to you: God is light; in him there is no darkness at all" (1 John 1:5 NIV).

WHOOSH! SMACK!

As I fight off the slow-motion effects of mining fatigue—inflicted by the laser zap of the elder guardian—Techgirl comes to the rescue.

SMACK! SMACK! SMACK!

She slays the creature, which drops two prismarine shards. And just as quickly as it strikes, the danger fades. We're safe again...basking in the warm glow of our jack-o'-lantern.

GAMEPLAY SECRETS

When the sun goes down, torches of every size and shape light up. During gameplay at night, players need a light source so they can continue the fun...and stay safe. Hostile monsters—spiders, creepers, zombies...even elder guardians—spawn in the dark. It has happened in my very own shelter, not to mention every temple and mine I've explored.

Dragee90's Best Tip

Always keep a light source in your inventory. Underwater? No problem. As you saw today, a handy jack-o'-lantern can light up any dark place. Glowstone can do the trick as well. Remember, light is your friend in Minecraft.

REAL-LIFE SECRETS

Read It

"Your word is a lamp that gives light wherever I walk" (Psalm 119:105).

Think It

How is the Bible like a lamp that guides us? What would happen if we never took the time to study or memorize Scripture?

Live It

Whether we're exploring mysterious passageways in Minecraft or setting off on a wilderness adventure in the real world, we need a bright torch that can light our way. Okay, maybe not the kind Indiana Jones uses. But a trusty flashlight will do! It's the same way with our faith. We need the light of God's Word to guide us through life—and help us avoid dark, scary places. There are a lot of things we wouldn't know without the Bible:

> what God is like
>
> His plan for humans, like you and me
>
> how much He loves us
>
> the right way to live on this planet
>
> anything about what will happen to us after death

Spend time reading a verse every day.

Jot a Thought or Dream Up a Minecrafty Masterpiece

SECRET 56

Favorite Finds When Trading with Villagers

I'm back in a plains biome, wandering through my favorite Hobbit-like village.

Everything looks just as it did the last time I was here. The streets are still buzzing with activity—chickens clucking, pigs wallowing, and the townsfolk milling about in every direction. A huge iron golem lumbers by...*again*. He's still on duty, protecting villagers from hostile mob attacks.

Isn't this the same dude who lumbered by the last time I was here?

"Ahh...the Shire," I tell myself. "Nothing changes in this one-horse town." Suddenly, a horse trots by. "Except for that. I don't remember ever seeing a horse in this village!"

Today, I'm looking for a librarian—a blocky, pixelated character sporting a white robe. "There's my bald-headed, wobbly-nosed man," I tell myself. *At least I think it's a man. You just never know in Minecraft.*

I check his menu and pinpoint what I need—an enchanted

book. "Yikes, your prices are high," I protest. "But I guess I have no choice…"

I stop in midsentence. I get that tingly, déjà vu feeling again, like I've uttered these very words before…in this very spot. Just then, a bat flutters through the rafters and then retreats to a dark corner.

"Okay…that's new too," I mumble. So far I've seen a horse and a bat. I look down at my Minecrafty skin. *Yep, still a duck. All is normal! Now, where was I? Oh yeah, the middle of an important trade…*

The librarian insists on a whopping 54 emeralds in exchange for the rare book. Frustration wells up inside, and I feel like arguing. But I hold my tongue. An important word pops in my head: *integrity.*

My dad once got into heated negotiations with villagers in a Panamanian jungle. He was there during a summer mission trip, spending some downtime shopping for handmade goods. At issue was a beautiful wool blanket that probably took someone a month to create. The price was right and Dad knew it, but he thought he could sweeten the deal. Instead, the whole thing soured, and the craftsmen ended up feeling very offended. The moral of the story: Be fair and walk with integrity in every situation. People are "reading" us.

I exchange the emeralds and collect the enchanted book.

A purple particle effect appears over the librarian's head, which means he's ready to wheel and deal on another trade—and this time he offers me a can't-miss bargain.

"Score," I say. "You're on, dude—let's keep trading."

Once again, that déjà vu feeling tingles through my body. *I guess I've said these words before—and probably will again…and again…and again…*

GAMEPLAY SECRETS

As I've said before (there I go again), emeralds are like currency in Minecraft. Players can trade these precious gems with villagers for other rare, valuable, and much-needed items. It's a fun feature of gameplay that makes this virtual world a bit more like the real one. You can trade with five kinds of villagers: farmers, priests, butchers, blacksmiths, and librarians. You'll recognize them by their clothing. To start a transaction, you select a villager, read their trading menu, and then exchange emeralds for the items you want.

Dragee90's Best Tip

Don't trade for items you can easily craft yourself—such as basic food (pork chops, for example) or tools (like a hoe or shovel). Instead, hold out for the rare finds: potions, enchanted books, ender pearls...okay, and maybe cake. I'd definitely trade an emerald for cake!

REAL-LIFE SECRETS

Read It

"You are our letter, and you are in our hearts for everyone to read and understand. You are like a letter written by Christ and delivered by us. But you are not written with pen and ink or on tablets made of stone. You are written in our hearts by the Spirit of the living God" (2 Corinthians 3:2-3).

Think It

How are we like a letter written by Christ? What do people "read" when they see your life?

Live It

One day, my dad looked me in the eye and asked, "Chris, when people see your 'life letter' do they read the name Jesus?" *Say what? Life letter? "Read" the name Jesus?* I was confused—

until I read 2 Corinthians 3:2-3. God doesn't want us to hide our faith from the world. He wants to shine so brightly through our lives that others can't help but see Him. How? Through our words, actions, and attitudes. Especially by being kind and doing our best to love others:

> Jesus replied: "'Love the Lord your God with all your heart and with all your soul and with all your mind.' This is the first and greatest commandment. And the second is like it: 'Love your neighbor as yourself'" (Matthew 22:37-39 NIV).

Also, God wants us to speak up instead of keeping quiet. "Always be prepared to give an answer to everyone who asks you to give the reason for the hope that you have" (1 Peter 3:15 NIV).

How to Defeat a **Wither**

A wither is the Frankenstein of Minecraft monsters.

Instead of spawning naturally in the game, it's created by players—and that's really strange when you stop and think about it. Basically, you assemble blocks of soul sand in the shape of a T and top it off with three wither skulls. But once all the parts come together, you'd better run. Your freshly made creature will flash blue and grow bigger right before your eyes.

And then...*BOOM!*

After a loud bang and a hideous shriek, a three-headed ghoul comes after you.

It's alive!

A wither is capable of destroying any block in its path, and it ruthlessly attacks other mobs—including players. So the question is, why create something that wants to eat you? My gaming friend Awesomecupcake didn't have a very good answer.

"Look, dude, I wasn't thinking," he blurts through his headset as we head for the hills in the Taiga M biome. Even though our legs are a blur, a wither is still gaining on us.

"I wasn't sure I could actually make one," my friend continues. "But it worked. And just look at that thing. It's so cool!"

Just then, all three wither heads fire deadly projectiles right at us.

"*No!*" I shout. "There's nothing cool about a wither...or this mess you got us in. Did you see what it fired at us? Actual skulls!"

The entire predicament feels a lot like some real-world trouble another friend got into. He and his buddy were stuck on the roof of a neighbor's shed...with an angry dog barking at them. It all started when one of the boys insisted they hop over a fence and cut through a yard to save time getting home. (Apparently they were late.) They knew better—they'd been told countless times not to go that route. But my friends took a chance, only to face their neighborhood wither—a 150-pound Great Dane. They emerged unbitten but learned a lesson the hard way: "Whoever walks with the wise becomes wise, but the companion of fools will suffer harm" (Proverbs 13:20 ESV).

"There's only one way to defeat this thing," Awesomecupcake tells me as we take cover on a rocky ledge.

"I'm all ears," I say.

"We wear full diamond armor and rev up everything with Projectile Protection enchantments—including our bows and arrows. I'll distract the wither by running, jumping, and dodging the projectiles. You attack with your bow."

I agree to the plan. "It's go time, dude."

GAMEPLAY SECRETS

As you just saw, this floating, three-headed mob is very difficult to defeat, not to mention very dangerous. Withers can move *very* quickly. And when they come at you, watch out. They attack with a projectile called a wither skull. If it strikes you, it inflicts what's called Wither II, which is sort of like a poison that can kill and turn your health bar back. Also, a wither is able to break any block in the game.

Dragee90's Best Tip

Wearing full diamond armor with Projectile Protection enchantments is the best hope of defeating a wither. Also, keep in mind that a wither can still see players who use the Potion of Invisibility. And watch out: A wither won't attack a zombie or a skeleton, so a whole army of these creatures could end up joining forces with a wither and set their sights on you!

REAL-LIFE SECRETS

Read It

"People who are ruled by their desires think only of themselves. Everyone who is ruled by the Holy Spirit thinks about spiritual things. If our minds are ruled by our desires, we will die. But if our minds are ruled by the Spirit, we will have life and peace. Our desires fight against God, because they do not and cannot obey God's laws. If we follow our desires, we cannot please God" (Romans 8:5-8).

Think It

What rules your mind—selfish thoughts or God-centered ones? And how good are your friendships? Do the kids you hang out with help you, or are you caught in the quicksand of bad company?

Live It

Friends. The *right* ones will get in your face when you're blowing it, pull you up when you're down, and even put your best interests before their own. And the wrong ones? Let's just say I've seen too many lives messed up because of stupid decisions—and the bad influence of lethal people. Building the right friendships and being the right kind of friend to others are important steps in growing a strong faith.

**Jot a Thought or Dream Up
a Minecrafty Masterpiece**

Wood—a Basic Resource That's Fun to Use

I'm covering the walls of Mount Quack's library with planks of dark oak. It looks so smart and stately—like the elegant libraries I've seen in English manors.

Unfortunately, Techgirl disagrees.

"There's way too much going on in this room," she says, quick to point out lots of mistakes she thinks I've made. "You've mixed dark oak wood with mossy cobblestone—even gold blocks. Can we say *tacky*?"

"Has someone been watching too much HGTV?" I ask.

"Don't even get me started on those ugly traps you placed in your corridors."

I ignore the criticisms and go to work making planks. First, I place dark oak blocks in my 3x3 crafting grid. Before I know it, I have four planks. (They appear in the box to the right.) Next, I move them to my inventory. Now I'm ready to build.

"Glowstone?" Techgirl complains. "Are you serious? Torches look so much better. They cast a warm glow, and I think..."

I can't help but drown out the chatter. My mind flashes to a real-world scene in which this same friend tried to advise me on my basketball skills. She criticized how I dribbled the ball and even how I made shots. But in a one-on-one game, she couldn't do any of the things she told me to do. The Bible says a few things about know-it-all attitudes: "Don't pick on people, jump on their failures, criticize their faults—unless, of course, you want the same treatment. That critical spirit has a way of boomeranging" (Matthew 7:1 MSG).

"Hey, Techgirl," I interrupt. "Take a look at my library now. It's finished."

She gasps. The room looks great—even with the eclectic mix of wood, rock, and gold. The dark oak adds the perfect touch. As for the glowstone...it brightens up my room perfectly.

"It's really nice, Dragee90," my friend admits. "I'm sorry I didn't believe you." She walks through the place inspecting everything. "Yeah, HGTV would be proud."

GAMEPLAY SECRETS

Obviously, wood is harvested from trees. Logs are needed to create wooden planks (sometimes referred to simply as planks). Birch trees produce logs of various colors, which makes this resource fun to build with. Oak, spruce, birch, acacia, and jungle are the basic logs players can craft with. Jungle is great to use for building chests, and dark oak or birch is great for the interior of your shelter.

Dragee90's Best Tip

As you add a wood block to your crafting grid, make sure you place it in the right pattern. The block should go in the center.

REAL-LIFE SECRETS

Read It

"You can see the speck in your friend's eye, but you don't notice the log in your own eye. How can you say, 'My friend, let me take the speck out of your eye,' when you don't see the log in your own eye? You're nothing but show-offs! First, take the log out of your own eye. Then you can see how to take the speck out of your friend's eye" (Matthew 7:3-5).

Think It

Have you ever criticized someone for the same thing you do? Are you a "convertible Christian"—someone who behaves one way at church but another way at school or with the team?

Live It

Lots of gadgets in life are convertible—cars, clothing, computers...even Christians. Yep, it's sad but true. The kinds of believers I'm talking about see all kinds of faults in others without realizing they have them too. Even worse, they act one way at church and at home, but then they transform into someone totally different when they're with the crowd. It's amazing to watch. Their faith zips up into a hidden part of their hearts, and then their mouths unsnap. Before you know it, an endless stream of sarcasms, put-downs, and judgmental jabs drop out. Convertible Christianity can be summed up with one word—*hypocrisy*. Are you guilty of fake faith? If so, it's time for a change.

Jot a Thought or Dream Up a Minecrafty Masterpiece

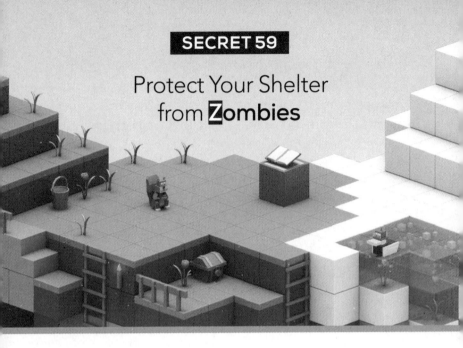

Protect Your Shelter from **Z**ombies

Techgirl may not like all the traps I've placed around Mount Quack, but they protect me from the monsters that roam in the night—especially from zombies.

Soul sand works well at slowing down these guys (flip back to Secret 51 for more about this trap). But the best defense is light.

AAARRRR!

They growl and moan as they come into contact with my torch or with a nice chunk of glowstone. They twist and squirm, clawing aimlessly at the air, and then they lumber back into the shadows. Light overcomes the darkness and keeps the monsters at bay, so I do two things with it:

I keep a torch in my hotbar while I'm outside. If daylight turns to darkness, I'm ready for zombies.

I torch up my shelter. Torches and glowstone are literally everywhere at Mount Quack—my corridors, my rooms, and especially in my mine.

Light comforts me in the real world too. Whenever I get scared as I lie in my bed, a nightlight gives me peace. And so does something else—prayer. The Bible says, "The light shines in the darkness, and the darkness has not overcome it" (John 1:5 NIV). It also says, "When Jesus spoke again to the people, he said, 'I am the light of the world. Whoever follows me will never walk in darkness, but will have the light of life'" (John 8:12 NIV).

It's dark outside, yet I'm walking confidently down the corridors of Mount Quack.

I zigzag past my traps and take comfort in all the torches. I'm even carrying one in my duck hands. I'm safe—because light overcomes the darkness. And that includes zombies.

GAMEPLAY SECRETS

A zombie is a hostile creature that only appears at night. It makes a groaning sound that is distinguishable from all other Minecraft mobs, and it fights at close range. Sunlight is a zombie's biggest enemy—it makes a zombie spontaneously burst into flames.

Dragee90's Best Tip

These clumsy green creatures come out only in the evening and gravitate to dark places, like caves and dungeons. They hate the light, which is why I make my shelter as bright as possible—inside and out. I also set traps that can hold a zombie until daybreak.

REAL-LIFE SECRETS

Read It

"Be on your guard and stay awake. Your enemy, the devil, is like a roaring lion, sneaking around to find someone to attack" (1 Peter 5:8).

Think It

Do we have the resources to out-muscle the devil's deadly schemes? If so, what are they and where do we find them?

Live It

The Bible uses different names to describe Satan: deceiver (Revelation 12:9 ESV), inciter (1 Chronicles 21:1 NIV), accuser (Zechariah 3:1), sinner (1 John 3:8), murderer and liar (John 8:44), to name a few. Scripture makes it clear that he is rotten to the core. The devil wants to make us enemies with God, and he uses every kind of distraction imaginable—boredom, selfish desires, inferiority, doubt, fear...the list could fill up this book! But here's some good news: Our Lord Jesus Christ is our ultimate ally—our ultimate defender. Jesus is stronger than the devil, and He protects us. But it's up to us to do a few things to resist the devil: pray to God daily, read the Bible, get involved in church, and learn to trust Jesus.

Watch Out for the Zombie-Pigman

I'm running for my life through the Nether.

But I got what I came for—nether quartz (so I can build cool stuff), netherrack (for my fireplaces), and glowstone (for lights at Mount Quack).

And I acquired something unexpected—an enchanted gold sword from a zombie-pigman. How'd I get it? Believe me, you don't want to know! But it involved a squeal and a *SWACK!*

Victory! I thought.

But then the creature's friends got pretty steamed and started chasing me. Unlike its counterparts in the Overworld, a zombie-pigman is pretty fast. Most of all, its scary appearance can paralyze you with fear. Imagine the green, slimy skin of a zombie mixed with the pink hide of a pig. Imagine horrifying, piglike faces with dark, dead eyes.

Actually—*don't* imagine them!

I covered my eyes when a scary scene filled my TV screen in

the real world. I was watching a spooky movie my mom warned me to avoid. I tried to change the channel, but then I was drawn into the action. And now some grotesque images are stuck in my brain. I should have listened to my mom. I should also have taken some instructions from God's Word:

> He who walks righteously and speaks uprightly, who despises the gain of oppressions, who shakes his hands, lest they hold a bribe, who stops his ears from hearing of bloodshed and shuts his eyes from looking on evil, he will dwell on the heights; his place of defense will be the fortresses of rocks; his bread will be given him; his water will be sure (Isaiah 33:15-16 ESV).

"Don't be scared...don't be scared," I tell myself as I run through the Nether. My only hope is to find my original portal and get out of this crazy place.

Suddenly, I'm surrounded...but I find the portal just in time. *I'm safe!*

GAMEPLAY SECRETS

The Nether is home to the zombie-pigman, which is half zombie, half pig. This mob is neutral, unlike all other mobs in the Nether. But like a zombie, it fights in what is known as a *melee style*—close hand-to-hand combat.

REAL-LIFE SECRETS

Read It

"The demons begged Jesus, 'If you force us out, please send us into those pigs!' Jesus told them to go, and they went out of the men and into the pigs. All at once the pigs rushed down the steep bank into the lake and drowned. The people taking care of the pigs ran to the town and told everything, especially what had happened to the two men" (Matthew 8:31-33).

Think It

Do you believe that Jesus has power over everything in the universe? (Please explain.) Do you believe He has the power to change your life for the better? (Why or why not?)

Live It

After Jesus cast out the demons we just read about, those evil beings met their demise when they entered a heard of pigs. Moral of the story: Don't mess with Jesus! Do you ever think Jesus is a passive, never-get-mad, Mr. Nice Guy? Don't! He is the powerful Son of God, who is in control of the entire universe. Remember this:

> He has power over His enemies.
>
> He has the power to lay down His life and the power to take it back again.
>
> He has the power to defeat Satan.
>
> He has the power to free us from sin.
>
> He has the power to create and to heal.
>
> He has the power to transform the lives of believers.

Jot a Thought or Dream Up a Minecrafty Masterpiece

ACKNOWLEDGMENTS

Tiffany Ross, MDiv, is Christopher's mom. She ensured that everything in Christopher's book is biblically accurate. In addition to knowing a lot about Christian theology, Tiffany is a writer, videographer, and children's ministry pastor. She has authored and coauthored six books—including *101 Ways to Strengthen the Parent-Child Connection* and *A Servant's Heart* (both from Barbour)—and is a former film production coordinator at Focus on the Family. Tiffany graduated cum laude from Nazarene Theological Seminary in Kansas City.

Kid Advisory Team

I'm so grateful for these 12 Minecraft players (and friends) who became my official Kid Advisory Team. They were the very best detectives ever, examining the illustrations, the stories and the lessons, and offering their insights and gaming expertise.

Abby, 13, Nebraska
Caleb, 11, Iowa
Cooper, 8, Missouri
Gus, 10, Texas
John, 10, Missouri
Katelyn, 11, Missouri
Nathan, 8, Missouri
Roman, 18, Texas
Serena, 11, Nebraska
Shiloh, 7, Missouri
Tyson, 16, California
Zach, 13, Nebraska

Quick Guide to Topics and Bible Verses

ABOUT THE AUTHORS

Michael Ross is Christopher's dad. He researched and wrote *Building Faith Block by Block*—under Christopher's watchful eye, of course. Michael is an award-winning author and the former editor of *Breakaway*, a national magazine for teen guys published by Focus on the Family. He is also the author, coauthor, and collaborator of more than 37 books for Christian families, including the Gold Medallion winner *BOOM: A Guy's Guide to Growing Up* (Tyndale), a bestselling devotional he coauthored with Tiffany, *Faith That Breathes* (Barbour), and a bestselling parenting guide: *What Your Son Isn't Telling You* (Bethany House). Michael is married to Tiffany. The Ross family lives in Saint Charles, Missouri.

Christopher Ross, 15, was born in Colorado Springs, Colorado, and is a diehard Broncos fan. Today, he is a gifted student in Saint Charles, Missouri, where he participates in Duke University's TIP program for academically gifted kids. Outside the classroom, he's a skilled lacrosse player, basketball fanatic, and adventure traveler. His favorite spring break was spent in the Bahamas, swimming with a dolphin named Shawn. During his summers, he likes to go white-water rafting in the Rockies. Christopher is a math-minded student who is creative, funny, and destined for cool opportunities in life. No doubt about it, this won't be his last book. As with his dad, the quest for a good story pulsates through his veins. When he isn't cracking the books or shooting hoops, he spends his time in the worlds of Minecraft.

Get Even More Minecraft
Tips and Tricks

Did you enjoy all the helpful hints in this book?
Dig deeper in your gaming experience
when you follow **Dragee90** on his YouTube channel.
Watch more Let's Play videos filled with new
tips and tricks you won't find in the book.

Look for **Dragee90** on YouTube and
level up your Minecraft game!

To learn more about Harvest House books and
to read sample chapters, visit our website:

www.harvesthousepublishers.com

HARVEST HOUSE PUBLISHERS
EUGENE, OREGON